101 FASCINATING CANADIAN Music FACTS

DAVID McPHERSON

101 FASCINATING CANADIAN Music FACTS

DUNDURN PRESS

Publisher: Kwame Scott Fraser | Acquiring editor: Kathryn Lane | Editor: Carrie Gleason
Cover designer: Karen Alexiou
Cover image: guitars: mochipet/istock.com; background: vda_82/shutterstock.com

Library and Archives Canada Cataloguing in Publication

Title: 101 fascinating Canadian music facts / David McPherson.
Other titles: One hundred one fascinating Canadian music facts | One hundred and one fascinating Canadian music facts
Names: McPherson, David (Music journalist), author.
Description: Series statement: 101 fascinating facts 2
Identifiers: Canadiana (print) 20230451616 | Canadiana (ebook) 2023046162X | ISBN 9781459751583 (softcover) | ISBN 9781459751606 (EPUB) | ISBN 9781459751590 (PDF)
Subjects: LCSH: Popular music—Canada—Miscellanea.
Classification: LCC ML3484 .M172 2023 | DDC 781.64/0971—dc23

  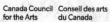

We acknowledge the support of the Canada Council for the Arts and the Ontario Arts Council for our publishing program. We also acknowledge the financial support of the Government of Ontario, through the Ontario Book Publishing Tax Credit and Ontario Creates, and the Government of Canada.

Dundurn Press
1382 Queen Street East
Toronto, Ontario, Canada M4L 1C9
dundurn.com, @dundurnpress 𝕏 f ◎

For Alex and Isabella

INTRODUCTION

As Canadians, we are lucky to call some of the greatest songwriters of the 20th century our own: from Gordon Lightfoot and Joni Mitchell to Leonard Cohen and Buffy Sainte-Marie. We are also fortunate to have a thriving music industry, which every day is helping to produce the next generation of stars.

Canadians have historically had an inferiority complex, comparing themselves to their southern neighbours. It has been a long-held notion — especially in the arts — that you only really *made it* when you made some noise and achieved success in the United States. Because of this, Canadians sometimes forget the incredible wealth of talent that their country has produced. How many times, in the course of a conversation with a friend about music, have you heard them reply, "I didn't know they were Canadian!"

This book allowed me to take a deeper look at some of the fascinating facts and extraordinary stories of Canadian artists I had forgotten, or I had yet to discover. There was no shortage of stories to choose from as I curated these 101 fascinating Canadian music facts. The challenge was making the difficult decision on what stories *not* to include. I wanted to make sure I had enough variety and diversity — in genre, in geography, and in the musicians featured in these pages. After pulling out these facts from my archives of past interviews, from new interviews, and from new research, I was left with an overwhelming feeling of patriotic pride for the incredible breadth of music our country has produced.

I was struck by the variety not only in genre but also in the talent that has come from coast to coast. There are so many behind-the-scenes stars you may not be aware of, like Grammy-winning producers and songwriters. In choosing the stories that made the final cut, I tried to reflect this variety. In the pages that follow you will read about a polka king and a hip-hop Guinness World Record holder. You will read about a Juno-nominated Cree musician, our first bona fide country music superstar, and the stories behind the genesis of some of your favourite songs.

Music is the elixir of life. Those six words will be etched on my tombstone. For more than 25 years now, I've been fortunate to combine my passion for music with writing. I've spent a quarter of a decade immersing myself in Canadian music by researching, listening, learning — and discovering — the rich history that exists. This journey started when I was a student at Western University. As a volunteer reporter for the university paper's arts section and later the entertainment editor, I discovered many Canadian artists and bands and watched as their careers took flight from playing the campus bar to packing stadiums across North America. Since then, I've been fortunate to share their stories with wider audiences of music lovers in a variety of North American publications and in a pair of books.

I am pleased that you now have a turn at discovering these fascinating facts for yourself. The stories are in no particular order. Feel free to read them at random and share them with others. I hope you enjoy reading this book as much as I enjoyed gathering these fascinating facts.

LUCKY LUTHIER

Flash back to 1976. Canadian guitar-maker Linda Manzer is 26 years old and heading to San Francisco with a friend. A pit stop in Marin County, in the Bay Area, proves lucky in unexpected ways.

Carlos Santana's drummer Graham Lear (an English-born Canadian) and his first wife, Sandra, (both friends of Manzer) lived in a guest house on the 10-time Grammy winner's property. Manzer met the legendary guitarist and spent a couple of nights with him before returning to Canada. Two months later, while continuing her tutelage on flattop guitar construction with master luthier Jean Larrivée in Victoria, British Columbia, a letter arrived from the Lears asking her to build a guitar for Santana as a Christmas gift.

Manzer accepted. She researched everything she could find about Santana, discovering he was a follower of the teachings of the Indian guru Sri Chinmoy and had recently changed his name to Devadip. Manzer made an inlay with this spiritual name, along with an om — the sacred symbol of Hinduism that represents inner peace. Before packaging the guitar and sending it to Graham and Sandra, Manzer played it to open it up. She was living with another couple who also worked for Larrivée, and they were playing John Denver's Christmas record non-stop. "I put that guitar up to the speakers as we listened," Manzer recalls. "If ever one can find Denver's influence in Santana's work, it would be because that is what the guitar started out listening to!"

Many months later, Manzer was reading a feature interview with Santana in *Guitar Player* magazine one afternoon and nearly fell out of her chair. The reason, the following sentence: "This friend of mine, Linda Manzer, made me a guitar with a really great tone!"

Those 15 words inked in print were life-changing and launched Manzer's career. Over the next 45 years, the master luthier (a skilled craftsperson who makes and repairs stringed instruments) designed guitars for everyone from Canadians Bruce Cockburn and Stephen Fearing to American jazz musician Pat Metheny. "I was just in the right place at the right time," she recalls. "People say you are not supposed to say you are lucky; you make your own luck, but I really feel like I've been incredibly lucky."

POWWOW BAND WOWS GRAMMYS

The story of the Indigenous music group Northern Cree began in 1982. The Wood brothers (Steve, Randy, Charlie, and Earl) from the Saddle Lake Cree Nation gathered and forged a plan to bring their traditional music to a larger audience beyond the boundaries of their reserve of Saddle Lake, Alberta.

Over the past 40 years they've succeeded. The band has swelled to 17 rotating members. They've released more than 20 albums and countless other live recordings. They've been nominated for nine Grammys and three Junos, and they've performed around the world.

"We've taken the powwow out of its traditional setting and put it on stage just like other music," explains Northern Cree co-founder Steve Wood. "When I was 14 years old, I attended my first-ever concert in Edmonton, Alberta, at the newly built Northlands Coliseum. We were on our way to a powwow in the south of Calgary and stopped in Edmonton. The artist was Kiss. I sat there watching Ace [Frehley] and the rest of the band playing that night and thought, 'Why can't we put our music on a stage like this?' I realized we could. It's just how you present it. I had a dream then and it has come to fruition. We've now performed in front of audiences up to 50,000."

Wood recalls attending the Grammys:

> The first time we attended the Grammy Awards, we had only ever seen them on TV before. We had never seen anything like it … all these people in penguin suits! What did we do? We copied them of course. We rented tuxedos and wore uncomfortable shoes. I didn't enjoy that, plus nobody spoke to us. So, the next time we attended, we decided to dress as ourselves. We wore ribbon shirts that were created by a Native designer to our first Grammy party. We were like magnets that night. People, out of the blue, kept coming up to us.
>
> I'll never forget that moment when our limo driver with the eight of us piled inside

pulled up to the red carpet. The usher came to the door, ready to greet us. Instead, our driver locks the doors. The ushers on the red carpet are looking through the windows trying to see who we were. We waited 45 seconds before unlocking the doors. We jumped out. All of us were wearing headdresses and the women were in beautiful beadwork. There was a huge crowd of photographers around a young lady ahead of us on the red carpet. One of the photographers notices us and begins snapping endless photos. Soon all the photographers notice us and move to where we are, leaving the young lady standing alone, off to the side. An usher tells her she needs to move. At that moment, the woman in front of us turns and says to one of the crew, "Who are you guys anyway?" They replied: "Northern Cree!" Then, my son turned to me and said, "Dad, that is Camila Cabello!"

We continued to walk along the red carpet and talk to some reporters. Then, a woman comes up to me and says, "My client wants to take a picture with you guys." I said no problem. You know who it was? Cyndi Lauper! I had listened to her all the time during my studies at the University of Saskatchewan. Cyndi says to me, "I've been here many times and you guys are the best dressed I've ever seen!"

While we may not have won a Grammy, we were already winners, making those connections that identifies, recognizes, and respects our ethnicity/culture.

In 2017, we opened the Grammy Awards in the afternoon, before the telecast, as the first official act. It was unbelievable! Later, I looked at all of the performers from that day and we had the most views, second only to Beyoncé. I didn't go to the evening ceremony. Instead I returned to our hotel, called my wife, and went to sleep. When I woke up, I looked at our YouTube page and read all of the comments about our performance. We had millions of hits on our page. Many of the comments were from our people across Turtle Island. One in particular stands out. The person wrote: "I was standing in front of the TV screen with my 86-year-old grandmother holding hands and we were both crying!" We had really done something huge for all our people.

OPERA SAVES HARD ROCKER'S VOICE

A classically trained opera singer, who once sang arias at Carnegie Hall, giving voice lessons to a rock 'n' roll star? Sounds like fantasy, but it's true.

Tenor Edward L. Johnson, born in Hamilton, Ontario, was the youngest member of the New York Metropolitan Opera company and a founding member of the Hamilton Opera Company. He was an in-demand opera star that sang on some of the biggest stages throughout North America.

In 1976, Johnson decided to retire from touring and settled in Fergus, Ontario, to focus on teaching the bel canto method, which translated means "beautiful singing." Johnson learned this Italian vocal technique, which dates back to the 15th century, from Giuseppe Giuffrida at the Metropolitan Opera.

Little known fact: many of Johnson's students were more apt to play blue-collar bars than soft-seat theatres. Brian Vollmer, lead singer of hard-rock band Helix, is one of these disciples; he credits Johnson with saving his voice and prolonging his career. Before taking lessons with Johnson, the singer was diagnosed with nodes on his vocal cords so bad that doctors told him if he continued to sing he would probably never be able to speak to his children. Instead of opting for surgery, Vollmer found Johnson.

"Ed was like a father to me," the Helix front man says. "He not only saved my voice, but he also taught me to be a teacher. Of all the students that he taught to be teachers, I was the only one he gave his blessing to. Why? Because I took almost every Monday for 16 years to drive from London to Fergus to not only take a lesson with him, but also to talk about the technique. Bel canto was largely passed down by word of mouth through the centuries. It's the only way to sing without tension on the vocal cords. However, very little was written down about the technique, which led to charlatan voice teachers claiming that they taught 'bel canto' when in reality they knew nothing about it."

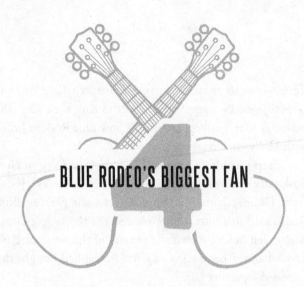

BLUE RODEO'S BIGGEST FAN

David Lee Roth (Van Halen's original lead singer) once saw Blue Rodeo perform at Toronto's Horseshoe Tavern. So did actor Tom Cruise. And while Canada's favourite roots-rockers never "made it" south of the border, they certainly had their share of celebrity fans. One of those American admirers led to the 11-time Juno Award–winning group from Toronto landing a gig in a Hollywood film.

Picture this. You are a rising Canadian band trying to make inroads in the United States. Your label (Atlantic Records) has you slogging the long and winding road stateside. Night after night you play sleazy bars in Texas towns and Florida watering holes to audiences who do not get your music. You wonder, is this worth it? Then, one night during a break in this monotony — at a dive bar in Austin,

Texas — a call comes from your manager telling you one of Hollywood's biggest stars wants to sing with you. The actress is Meryl Streep, and this is how Blue Rodeo's brush with Hollywood happened.

Streep was filming the dark comedy *She-Devil* in New York City and commuting into the Big Apple every day from Connecticut. Her limo driver kept playing Blue Rodeo's debut album, *Outskirts*, and the three-time Oscar winner fell in love with it. At the end of the week, Streep's driver handed her a copy of *Outskirts* he had bought the actress as a parting gift.

Flash ahead to Streep's next project, *Postcards from the Edge* — a semi-autobiographical screenplay written by Carrie Fisher and directed by Mike Nichols (*Who's Afraid of Virginia Woolf?*, *Working Girl*, *The Birdcage*). Nichols gave Streep a stack of cassettes to listen to and pick a band to feature in the film. Among them was Blue Rodeo's sophomore record, *Diamond Mine*. Streep remembered the band and, without listening to any of the other tapes, said, "Get these guys!"

Blue Rodeo were invited to audition at Toronto's Diamond Club during the Toronto International Film Festival (TIFF). Streep and Nichols did not have a movie at TIFF that year, so the media were left wondering why the pair were in town. After hearing the roots-rockers play, Nichols and Streep were sold. "See you in L.A.!" Streep said as she left the Diamond; the boys in the band were stunned as the whole experience still felt surreal.

The next thing they knew, the band was on a movie set in Burbank, California, with Streep, Shirley MacLaine, and Dennis Quaid. Blue Rodeo accompanied Streep as her wedding band in *Postcards from the Edge.* They played the Shel Silverstein–penned "I'm Checkin' Out," which was nominated for an Academy Award in the Best Original Song category in 1990 and performed by Reba McEntire at the Oscar ceremonies the following year.

AUDITIONING FOR A BEACH BOY

On October 6, 2004, Brian Wilson, co-founder of the Beach Boys, was in Toronto to play the famed *Smile* record, which had been scrapped back in the late 1960s and released by Wilson as *Brian Wilson Presents Smile* in 2004. The venue: Massey Hall. Early in the afternoon, the songwriter taped an interview in the seats on the mezzanine level with Peter Mansbridge for CBC's *The National*. Wilson then joined his band onstage for sound check. Rather than run through the songs in the set, Wilson wanted them to learn a new composition he had apparently written in his hotel room earlier that day. Steve Waxman, vice-president of publicity at Warner Music Canada, watched from the seats as the band gathered to hear the song and observe the chords Wilson played on the piano. The musicians returned to their designated spots and Wilson then walked from one player to another instructing them on what parts he wanted them to play. Waxman recalls how amazing it was to witness this song come to life in front of his eyes. After three or four takes of the song, the sound check finished, and the band left the stage.

Waxman headed to Wilson's dressing room to get him to sign some posters and found him sitting at a keyboard still practising the song. Curious, the record executive asked the former Beach Boy if he planned to play the new song that night. Wilson replied that he hadn't decided yet. And then, much to Waxman's surprise, he asked, "Do you know how to sing?" Waxman insisted he had a lousy voice, but Wilson replied, "Everybody can sing!" Wilson asked if Waxman thought he could remember the melody of the new song. A musician who played guitar and had worked in the music industry for more than two decades by this time, Waxman figured he could do it. Wilson handed him the handwritten lyrics and started to play the tune on the keys.

"I tried my hardest not to butcher the song," Waxman recalls. "In the end, Brian smiled and said to me, 'Well, you could be in the choir!'"

Wilson didn't play the song that night at Massey Hall, and Waxman hasn't heard it since — but that dressing room audition with the legendary Beach Boy is a music memory he'll never forget!

"SNOWBIRD" TAKES FLIGHT

Today, Canadians use the word "snowbird" to refer to retirees migrating south to warmer climes for the winter. Back in 1970, "Snowbird" was the title of one of the world's most popular songs. First released in 1969 on Anne Murray's *This Way Is My Way*, it wasn't until the following summer that the ballad — written in just 25 minutes by a folk and country songwriter born in Val-d'Or, Quebec, named Gene MacLellan — was discovered, thanks to an American DJ who played the B-side of Murray's record. This beautiful folk song struck a chord. With its poetic words and singalong melody, it changed forevermore the lives of both Murray and MacLellan. A crossover hit, "Snowbird" reached No. 2 on Canada's pop charts and No. 1 on both the adult contemporary and country charts. South of the border, "Snowbird" reached No. 8 on the U.S. pop singles chart, spent six weeks at No. 1 on the adult contemporary chart, and even cracked country radio's Top 10.

The song — only the second composition MacLellan ever wrote — earned the songwriter a Juno Award for Composer of the Year and a BMI Award as the first Canadian composer with a song played more than one million times in the U.S. On the strength of the song's success, Murray became the first solo female artist in Canadian history to receive an American gold record for sales over one million. From Bing Crosby to Chet Atkins, more than a hundred other artists have covered the song. "Snowbird" even resonated with international audiences. European musicians recorded versions in Czech, German, Swedish, Italian, Flemish, and other languages. In 2003, the song was inducted into the Canadian Songwriters Hall of Fame.

Here's how this MacLellan masterpiece arrived in Murray's hands and became a hit. The Nova Scotia songwriter was guesting on *Don Messer's Jubilee* and Bill Langstroth, who Murray later married, was the show's producer. After hearing MacLellan perform "Snowbird," Bill called Murray and said, "You have to hear the songs this guy has!" Murray went down to the CBC building in Halifax and listened to a tape of a few of Gene's songs in the conference room. Afterwards, she asked the songwriter if she could take the tape and have the songs. MacLellan agreed.

Murray recorded a pair of MacLellan's songs ("Just Bidin' My Time" and "Snowbird") on her 1969 release, *This Way Is My Way*. Back then, records had A-sides and B-sides. "Just Bidin' My Time" was the A-side; "Snowbird" the B-side. One day, a DJ in Cleveland, Ohio, flipped over the record and played "Snowbird" on the air. Listeners responded and other stations picked up the song. That American DJ's decision changed Murray's life.

"'Snowbird' was the song that started it all," says Murray. "It was the one, no matter how many hits I had, that people always went back to ... it absolutely changed my life! A lot of people never have a hit record, but to have that as your first, and have it achieve what it did, was pretty amazing."

LOVE BY THE LAKE

A summer tradition unlike any other: listening to live music outdoors on the shores of Lake Ontario. Toronto's Ontario Place Forum opened in 1971 and was demolished in 1994 to be replaced with the Molson Amphitheatre (now Budweiser Stage). In 1976, a revolving stage was added to the Forum and artists that performed there over its lifespan ranged from classical to rock, blues to country, and all genres in between, including countless Canadian acts.

Here's a fun fact! The Forum is where American musician Lyle Lovett and actress Julia Roberts publicly announced their engagement during his encore. The night of this unlikely proposal was June 24, 1993. It was the early days of the internet and before ubiquitous cellphone use.

Nobody knew Lovett and Roberts were an item. Partway through the show, Lovett's tour manager came to Jennifer Johnston, a student working a summer job at the Forum, and said, "Lyle needs a cellphone right away. His girlfriend is going to call him shortly and she has a small window to talk." Johnston explained the unusual request to her manager, who passed on Ontario Place's cellphone with a stern warning: "If you lose this it's your ass, kid!"

Johnston was instructed to take the call and wait for Lovett to finish his set. The call came. Oblivious as to who was on the other end of the line, Johnston made small talk with Lovett's girlfriend. When the singer came backstage, he grabbed the phone, and a few seconds later told Johnston to bring the phone and follow him onstage for his encore.

Lovett stepped up to the microphone. With a wide-eyed smile, he announced to the sold-out crowd: "I just found out I'm going to get married!" The audience went wild. The singer-songwriter then played a song for his fiancée while Johnston held the phone.

After this memorable night, Johnston had a few days off. On her second day at home, she was snoozing in bed shortly after 8 a.m. when her phone started ringing off the hook. "Everybody knows I'm not a morning person, but I had five calls in a row telling me it was Julia Roberts I was talking to!" Johnston recalls. The story of Lovett and Roberts's unlikely romance and quick nuptials (they had dated for just three weeks before announcing their marriage) was in all the papers that day. That summer, Roberts had been in Toronto filming *The Pelican Brief*. During a break in filming, the pair took advantage of the brief window to get married on June 27 in Marion, Indiana. The marriage only lasted 21 months, but the Ontario Place Forum, Toronto, and Johnston will forever be part of this piece of music history.

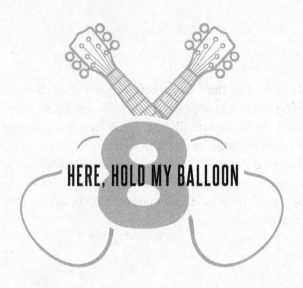

HERE, HOLD MY BALLOON

Sex? Check.

Drugs? Check.

Rock 'n' roll? Check.

Colour-coded love balloons to identify your status in the pickup game? Check.

The result: Lulu's Roadhouse, which for a period also held the record as the world's longest bar.

Located just off the highway outside Kitchener, Ontario, the 75,000-square-foot saloon named after a 1920s honky-tonk song opened on April 3, 1984. Its heyday was the mid- to late '80s when the Lulu's Roadhouse Band (led by Peter Padalino, who was also part of Major Hoople's Boarding House) played two sets a night to between 2,500 and 5,000 people, five nights a week. If you wanted 1960s nostalgia, this was the place. Acts booked included early American rock 'n' roll pioneers like Chuck Berry, Roy Orbison, Fats Domino, Jerry Lee Lewis, and Chubby Checker. Saturday nights were the busiest — and liveliest — and it was not uncommon for the bar to serve up to 25,000 drinks.

Lulu's was the brainchild of entrepreneur Karl Magid, who turned an old Kmart store into a palace of debauchery and dancing. When it opened, the tavern held the Guinness World Record for the world's longest bar (333.33 feet) and hosted a who's who of musical legends, not to mention countless late-night trysts and one-night stands.

Buses and limos rolled down the highway and into the packed parking lot from as far away as Buffalo with party-goers looking for a good time. That's where the balloons came in. For $1.50, patrons at Lulu's could purchase one of these colourful balloons and not worry about having to rehearse a lame pickup line. Red meant you were an available woman — ready to dance and party; blue meant the same for men; white indicated you were a virgin; yellow indicated you were shy; silver that you wanted to get lucky. And, finally, purple meant you were "hot and horny."

Kenny Hollis was a fixture in these early days of the famous roadhouse. The co-founder of Copperpenny, a rock band from Kitchener formed in 1968, he was the bar's tuxedo-clad emcee and schmooze king. After a couple of ownership changes, a reduction in size, and a change in musical mandate, Lulu's closed for good on April 8, 2000. Souvenir bricks from the once-legendary bar were sold off to memento seekers for $15 apiece or two for $25.

SPINNING WHEEL STILL PAYS BILLS

Step back in time to Toronto in the late 1960s.
The Yorkville neighbourhood's folk scene is at its peak.
Wandering the streets of this hippie haven, you might sight
Neil Young, Joni Mitchell, or John Kay (from Steppenwolf)
sipping coffee at venues like the Penny Farthing.

This milieu fuelled songwriter David Clayton-Thomas's
muse. His band, the Bossmen, had a number one hit single
called "Brain Washed" in Canada on Roman Records, but despite this commercial success, he was still playing the same folk
clubs in Yorkville and bars along Yonge Street like the Friar's
Tavern and Le Coq d'Or. Unfortunately, Roman Records filed
for bankruptcy. Clayton-Thomas was left to plot what next?

The songwriter signed with Arc Records and the label
gave him $500 to cut a few songs. So Clayton-Thomas went

back to his north Toronto apartment and wrote a composition called "Spinning Wheel" in just 15 minutes. It was a song that captured the zeitgeist of the late '60s. Clayton-Thomas was inspired by Dylan, who was the first songwriter he had heard that was writing rock 'n' roll songs that addressed societal issues. According to the songwriter, "'Spinning Wheel' was a protest song framed inside a happy, bouncy melody. In the late 1960s, everybody was getting carried up in all these movements … revolution was going on. I was telling people that everything is going to come full circle, don't get carried away with these movements. And, we saw that. We went in a span of five years from anti–Vietnam War protests to Ronald Reagan. The whole thing flipped on its head. The tune turned out to be prophetic." But Arc Records, who wanted another "Brain Washed," didn't see it that way, and dropped him.

Disenchanted with the Toronto scene and his prospects for commercial success, Clayton-Thomas packed his bags — including his demo — and headed to New York to try his luck. There, he started gigging at various Greenwich Village clubs. Folk singer Judy Collins heard him perform and told her friend Bobby Colomby (drummer for Blood, Sweat & Tears) about this new talent. As fate would have it, the band was on the lookout for a new vocalist. Clayton-Thomas got the job. When the band was working on their first record together, Clayton-Thomas played "Spinning Wheel" for

Fred Lipsius, the band's saxophonist and chief arranger. Lipsius loved it but suggested adding horns to replace some guitar lines. In 1969, the song was released as a single and peaked at No. 2 on the Billboard Hot 100. The album the single appeared on (the self-titled *Blood, Sweat & Tears*) sold 10 million copies worldwide and won five Grammy Awards. More than 400 artists — from James Brown doing an instrumental version to Sammy Davis Jr. — have covered the song in 20 different languages.

Today, 50 years on, the protest song written in a Toronto apartment in 15 minutes still pays David Clayton-Thomas's bills.

TWO SONGS FOR THE PRICE OF ONE

Songs, according to Burton Cummings, are "a valued commodity." The former lead singer of the Guess Who knows a bit about what makes a great song. As songwriters, Cummings and his long-time creative partner Randy Bachman were influenced by Buddy Holly, Ritchie Valens, the Beatles, and famed partnerships in song like Pomus and Shuman, and Bacharach and David. "They were all heroes to us," Cummings says. "Randy and I would always say to each other, 'Man, wouldn't it be something to be like one of those songwriting teams?' We never achieved their level, but some of the songs we wrote have never gone away, so that says something."

The Guess Who penned *many* songs that never went away. One such composition — inducted into the Canadian

Songwriters Hall of Fame in 2005 and released in 1970 — is actually two songs in one: "No Sugar Tonight/New Mother Nature." Bachman penned "No Sugar Tonight" and Cummings wrote "New Mother Nature."

"Randy had most of 'No Sugar Tonight' and I had 'New Mother Nature,'" Cummings recalls. "For some reason they were both in the key of F#, which is not a common compositional key. We showed each other these songs and discovered the symbiosis one morning at my grandmother's house in Winnipeg, where we often gathered to collaborate. Later, when we went into RCA Records studio on North Wacker Drive in Chicago to record *American Woman*, our producer, Jack Richardson, suggested squashing them together."

The inspiration for "New Mother Nature," came to Cummings in a pot-filled haze.

> I was hanging out with this Toronto band, the Rifkin, who later changed their name to Buckstone Hardware. Their bass player was named Jocko and that is where that line in the song comes from ["Jocko says yes and I believe him"]. During my hippy days, we used to party in the basement of my friend Chuck's parents ... hang out smoking joints, drinking beers, and listening to music — mostly the Doors and the Beatles. I always

have fond memories from those early days in
my career hanging out there.

The inspiration behind "No Sugar Tonight" is a bit
more colourful. Bachman remembers this story like it was
yesterday, even though it happened more than 50 years
ago. In 1969, the Guess Who was offered a four-city West
Coast tour opening for Frank Zappa and the Mothers of
Invention, along with a young Alice Cooper. The final gig
was in San Francisco on a Sunday night. The next morning, the band wandered the streets of Haight-Ashbury and
Telegraph Avenue in Berkley looking to find the epicentre
of hippie culture.

After shopping for some bootleg vinyl in the head shops
along Telegraph Avenue, Bachman went to put his purchases in the van they had parked on a side street. The songwriter recalls the scene that ensued:

> Suddenly, three guys with bulging muscles
> and tattoos start coming down the hill to-
> wards me: one black, one Chicano, and one
> white. These guys looked like biker gangs
> I had seen in movies … like the beginning
> of *Gunsmoke*. I was like, "What am I going
> to do?" Then I hear a car roaring up. It was
> brown with a blue door, a bumper hanging

off and dragging its muffler. Two of the three guys run. Now there is just me and one guy left. Out of the car gets this five-foot woman who starts screaming, "You no good so and so, you are supposed to be looking for a job, not sitting in a coffee shop and hanging out with your boys! You left me alone again with the kids." The guy gets in the car and she slams the door. The last thing I heard her say before she drove away was: "And furthermore, baby, when we get home, you ain't getting no sugar tonight!" I had never heard that phrase before. Immediately, I got in my car and wrote the skeleton of the song on a pad of paper.

When "American Woman" was released as a single, producer Jack Richardson, unbeknownst to Cummings, decided to put "No Sugar Tonight" on the flip side (i.e., without "New Mother Nature"). This caused a riff for a while between the songwriters. The double-sided single record *American Woman/No Sugar Tonight* peaked at No. 1 on the RPM charts and No. 1 on the Billboard Hot 100. Cummings got some retribution a few years later when fellow RCA recording artists the Friends of Distinction cut a funky R&B version of "New Mother Nature" without

"No Sugar Tonight." "I was very happy about that," he says. "In the long run, choosing Randy's song for the B-side of *American Woman* was a good move commercially, but at the time, it broke my heart."

YOU'LL HAVE TO EXCUSE ME ...

Canadian Gen-Xers know the lyrics to Spirit of the West's "Home for a Rest" well. They screamed them at the top of their lungs with best buddies in their college days. They danced wildly at friends' weddings to the song after a few too many libations, yelling lines like "You'll have to excuse me, I'm not at my best!" while sweat flew from their smiling faces. This party anthem was inducted into the Canadian Songwriters Hall of Fame in 2018. The song began as scribblings in band co-founder Geoffrey Kelly's journal. It's hard to imagine, but the rip-roaring tune that CBC Radio once named the 22nd Greatest Canadian Song of all time almost did not make the band's 1990 platinum release *Save This House*. Here's the backstory.

Save This House was recorded at Barney Bentall's Vancouver studio with award-winning producer Danny Greenspoon. With pre-production done, and most of the tracks picked, Greenspoon had his bags packed and was heading to the airport. Before leaving, he paused and asked the band if they had any more songs. Kelly offered what he called a "half-baked idea for a tune" and played the producer a bare-bones "Home for a Rest" on his acoustic guitar.

"Home for a Rest" started as a long poem written years before when Spirit of the West was schlepping across the U.K. playing pubs along Charing Cross Road like the Spice of Life and travelling with all their gear from town to town via buses, taxis, and trains. During this exhausting six weeks, the band spent most of the time crashing on friends' floors or cramming into a single hostel room.

Never a commercial radio hit, but somehow, organically via college radio and through Spirit of the West's spirited live shows, the song took on a life of its own and became the crowd-pleaser that ended shows with everyone pogo dancing.

Kelly admits the song was "a passport" for the band. "That one song was nearly enough to get us places," he says. "We had to back it up with other material, but it certainly helped to open the doors and gave us a little credibility. Every once in a while, I'll think about that song and relive that time when I wrote those lyrics. There is a charm in them that I love, like that verse about trains and travelling Yorkshire's green fields … I can still smell the hops in the air. It's a real snapshot of our early days as a band and a great little memento from that time."

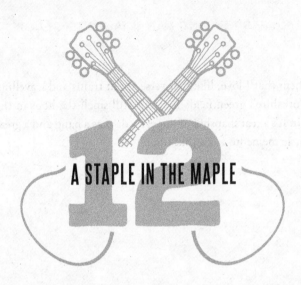

12

A STAPLE IN THE MAPLE

"Let Your Backbone Slide" was the first rap song inducted into the Canadian Songwriters Hall of Fame, and a huge hit for one Wesley Williams, better known as Maestro Fresh Wes. Here's how this hip-hop hit was born.

Williams was working security at Parkway Mall in Scarborough, Ontario, when one night during a regular shift he heard Billy Squier's hit "The Stroke." For some reason, the chorus resonated with Wesley. Something about the lines felt funky; they sounded like something James Brown might say. Before his shift ended, the Maestro decided to craft the song called "Let Your Backbone Slide."

Producers and co-writers Anthony and Peter Davis (First Offence Productions), who Williams met while attending Senator O'Connor College School in Scarborough, recorded a demo of the song at Don Valley Sounds in Markham, Ontario, and performed it on *Electric Circus* — a live dance and music program that aired on MuchMusic from the late 1980s until the early 2000s. Stevie B, a rising American singer-songwriter and record producer, who also owned a small indie label (LMR) was in the audience and signed the Maestro to his label.

Released in early 1990 as the lead single on the Maestro's debut, *Symphony in Effect*, "Let Your Backbone Slide" climbed the charts. By February of that year, it was No. 1 on RPM's Canadian Dance/Urban Music chart for three weeks — topping Janet Jackson, Paula Abdul, and 2 Live Crew. It was also No. 10 on the Top Singles chart that March. In the United States, "Let Your Backbone Slide" rose to No. 14 on Billboard's Rap Singles chart. The song was the first Canadian hip-hop single to go gold (50,000 units sold) and was nominated for five Juno Awards. In 1991, the hit took home a pair: the first-ever in the category Best Rap Recording of the Year and Best Video of the Year.

The song is now enshrined in Canadian hip-hop history. Or, as Williams says, "I have a slogan: 'Don't make records; make history.' That song ['Let Your Backbone Slide'] is a staple in the maple."

SONG HISTORIAN

A beloved folk musician who died far too young, Stan Rogers wrote songs that painted images of our home and native land one verse and one chorus at a time. In an early 1980s interview with American magazine *Folk Scene*, the songwriter spoke about his role as a song historian: "I hit upon the idea of taking my music in a kind of historical context, looking at the history of my country and its relationship to the rest of the world, and I started to write songs that reflected a kind of Canadian spirit."

Born and raised in Hamilton, Ontario, Rogers spent his summers in Nova Scotia. Rogers taught himself to play guitar on an instrument made by his uncle. His first gig was at Ebony Knight coffee house in Hamilton covering songs by Jimmie Rodgers, who is widely acknowledged as the

"Father of Country Music." Stan Rogers's pay: five bucks. Later, Rogers did some demos with producer Daniel Lanois at his Hamilton studio. The result of these sessions was his debut, *Fogarty's Cove*, released in 1977 on Mitch Podolak's independent label Barn Swallow Records.

History excited Rogers and he shared this passion and curiosity for the past with others through his songs. One of his most famous examples is "Northwest Passage" — a song about early explorers trying to discover a route across Canada to the Pacific Ocean. The song appeared on Rogers's 1981 album of the same name. Rogers's later records were financed by his mom, Valerie, and released independently on his own label, Fogarty's Cove Music. Unfortunately, Rogers became part of Canadian history himself when he made the news for his untimely death. While returning home from the Kerrville Folk Festival in Texas on June 2, 1983, Rogers died as the result of a fire on board Air Canada Flight 797 on the ground at the Greater Cincinnati Airport. He was 33 years old. In 2021, Rogers was honoured on a commemorative Canadian stamp. Today, the songwriter's memory is kept alive via an annual folk festival in Canso, Nova Scotia.

STOMPIN' TOM'S STOMPIN' BOARD

Charles Thomas Connors, a singer-songwriter raised in Skinners Pond, Prince Edward Island, left home at age 15 to hitchhike across Canada. Connors worked part-time jobs wherever he could find paid labour, writing songs all the while on his guitar. His first musical break came in Timmins, Ontario, while working in a local gold mine. Someone heard him sing and offered him a job playing at the Maple Leaf Hotel.

From these earliest gigs, Tom wore his trademark cowboy boots and stomped the heel of his left boot to keep rhythm. The faster the songs got, the louder and harder the stomps became. The nickname Stompin' Tom was born. The first time this moniker was used was in 1967 during Tom's introduction at a Centennial Day concert at the King George Tavern in Peterborough, Ontario.

The country singer stomped so hard that several bars and hotels complained about the damage he was doing to their stages and carpets. A few of them even kicked him out! So Connors came up with a simple solution — he started to bring his own piece of plywood to each gig. These three-foot by two-foot "stompin' boards" became Connors's trademark, along with his black Stetson. During the latter part of his career, in the 1990s, Tom always auctioned off one of these boards bearing his signature and donated the proceeds to a local charity. Today, an autographed board is on permanent display at Studio Bell at the National Music Centre in Calgary, Alberta.

HOW 'BOUT THEM APPLES?

Road Apples, the Tragically Hip's follow-up album to *Up to Here*, contains such Hip classics as "Three Pistols," "Little Bones," and "Twist My Arm." The band's lead singer, Gord Downie, was well-known for his poetic and cryptic lyrics, which makes one wonder what's behind the title to the Canadian rock band's sophomore major-label release.

It's actually a pretty funny story.

The band had several titles chosen but their American label (the Hip were signed directly to MCA Records in the U.S.) felt all of them were too much inside jokes or sounded "too Canadian," meaning that Americans would not understand the title. That's when the Hip — being the Hip — suggested *Road Apples*. The music industry execs loved it for its simplicity, thinking that the title just meant songs the band had written on the road. But unbeknownst to them, the phrase is an old American slang term that originated in the mid-20th century and refers to horse dung left behind on the road. The irony is the Tragically Hip had fooled the suits at MCA with their "inside joke." As drummer Johnny Fay recalled when chatting with the *Toronto Sun* on the record's 30th anniversary: "We were just making fun of ourselves ... before people reviewed it, we could beat them to the punch. 'Well,' we could say, 'It's horse shit!'"

16

ROLLIN' ON A ROLLIN' TRAIN

Toronto, 1970. After playing a show at the Canadian National Exhibition Grandstand, a group of the biggest names in music of that era boarded a chartered CN Railway train 14 cars long at Union Station. The idea: rather than have artists fly between shows, put them all on a party train that would allow them to get to know one another and jam between stops.

While financially a flop, the Transcontinental Pop Festival, or "Festival Express," was historic. It was the brainchild of twentysomething Toronto-based concert promoter Ken Walker. Four shows were scheduled: one in Toronto, one in Winnipeg, and two in Calgary. In between concerts, the train rattled westward from June 27 to July 5, carrying such acts as Janis Joplin and her Full Tilt Boogie

Band, Delaney & Bonnie, Buddy Guy, Eric Andersen, the Flying Burrito Brothers, Mountain, and the Grateful Dead. Canadian performers included Ian & Sylvia, the Good Brothers, and Rick Danko of the Band (the rest of the group decided to travel by plane to each show).

The Toronto stop was a two-day affair that ran from noon until midnight at the CNE Grandstand. Tickets cost $9 for one day or $14 for a two-day pass. The Toronto show was not without controversy. Mounted police and rowdy hippies clashed outside the CNE gates. These fans felt the show should be free. A compromise was reached to quell the rabble-rousers when the Dead's Jerry Garcia suggested they perform a free rehearsal set in nearby Coronation Park.

A poster for the Winnipeg stop on Canada Day promised "12 solid hours of soul-splitting, mind-bending glad vibrations and happy scenes by the greatest collection of rock, pop, and folk artists to ever appear here." Despite the hype, only about 4,600 concertgoers turned out in "the Peg" due to a number of external factors, including a Manitoba Centennial appearance by Prime Minister Pierre Elliott Trudeau.

The debauchery was legendary. So were the jams. Walker had made sure the train was equipped with sound systems. As the train rolled on, the musicians drank the bar dry and took copious amounts of drugs. Wanting to keep the party going, a hat was passed around to collect money to buy more booze. As seen in one famed scene about the all-star rock tour in the documentary *Festival Express*, the train made an unscheduled stop in Saskatoon and bought out most of the local store.

The July 4–5 Calgary stop was actually a last-minute addition. Originally, the tour was set to end in Vancouver, but this was changed due to a scheduling conflict at the Pacific National Exhibition. The pair of final Festival Express concerts occurred at McMahon Stadium on the University of Calgary campus; it's estimated 20,000 people attended. The first night the artists arrived in the city, some hijinks occurred — Janis Joplin allegedly flashed her tattooed breasts at a *Calgary Herald* reporter, goading him to take a picture, and Ian Tyson was attacked outside the Cecil Hotel and broke his hand fighting off the mugger.

The Canadian shows were also notable as some of Janis Joplin's final performances, as "Pearl" tragically died of a heroin overdose just two months later.

HUMBLE BEGINNINGS IN "THE HAMMER"

In 1976, Daniel Lanois, his brother Bob, and a friend named Bob Doidge who had played in bands with Dan in high school felt it was time to take their recording studio to the next level. The trio had been making records in a home-built studio known as Master Sound Recording in the Lanois brothers' mom's basement in Hamilton, Ontario. With the help of a loan, they purchased an Edwardian home on Grant Avenue and the famed studio of the same name was born.

The idea of building a studio in a house was pretty revolutionary at that time. It was here that future Grammy-winning producer and sonic sound chaser Daniel Lanois honed his craft. Some of the earliest recordings produced at Grant Avenue Studio included Canadian artists such as

Raffi, Willie P. Bennett, Parachute Club, Stan Rogers, and Gordon Lightfoot. In the early years, Daniel Lanois helped finance the studio by taking gigs as a guitarist in show bands and singing jingles on radio stations to help promote their fledgling business. In the 1980s, after Lanois set his sights outside Canada and started collecting Grammy Awards — working with the likes of U2, Peter Gabriel, Bob Dylan, Willie Nelson, Emmylou Harris, and others — Doidge took over running the studio. Today, Doidge remains involved as one of the studio's go-to in-house producers and recording engineers while the new ownership group makes sure Grant Avenue Studio maintains the Lanois brothers' home-studio philosophy and the essence of creating albums in an intimate setting.

CANADA'S NO. 1 COUNTRY BOY

How did a poor boy named Clarence Eugene
Snow (better known as Hank Snow), born on May 9, 1914,
in a quiet fishing village on Nova Scotia's South Shore, become an international country music star selling over 70
million records?

Easy: one number one song at a time, many written
from his first-hand adventures riding the rails and working
a variety of blue-collar jobs, from fishing boat cabin boy to
woodcutter.

Snow bought his first guitar, a T. Eaton Special, for
$5.95 from an Eaton's catalogue with earnings from his
cabin boy job when he was 12 years old. Jimmie Rodgers
was Hank's idol and the earliest songs he played during
his teenage years were covers of Rodgers's songs. (The

songwriter even named his only son Jimmie Rodgers Snow after this musical idol.)

The country and western singer's professional debut came in 1933 when Snow landed his own radio show and changed his on-air name from the Cowboy Blue Yodeler to Hank. In 1936, he recorded his first songs on RCA Victor's Bluebird label and signed a contract that lasted 47 years — the longest continuous contract in the history of the recording industry.

"I'm Movin' On" is one of Snow's most famous and treasured songs; the story is reminiscent of Jimmie Rodgers's train songs and describes the life of a restless wanderer who rides the rails across the land, never staying in one place for too long — a life familiar to Snow, especially during his early career. Released on May 5, 1950, "I'm Movin' On" was the first of seven No. 1 Billboard country hits Snow had in his long career. This song was the top country song of 1950 and stayed at number one for 21 consecutive weeks — a record Snow held, along with Webb Pierce's "In the Jailhouse Now" and Eddy Arnold's "I'll Hold You in My Heart (Till I Can Hold You in My Arms)," for over 60 years until it was surpassed by Florida Georgia Line's song "Cruise" in 2013. Snow also held another record (this one for 26 years) as the oldest country artist to score a number one single when his "Hello Love" hit the top of the charts in April 1979 when the artist was 59.

A diverse range of artists — from the Rolling Stones to Tina Turner and Ray Charles — have covered "I'm Movin' On." Its success led Snow to join the Grand Ole Opry and allowed the songwriter to buy his first home outside Nashville, Tennessee, dubbed Rainbow Ranch. Today, the Hank Snow Home Town Museum in Liverpool, Nova Scotia, a train stop away from his hometown of Brooklyn, is open year-round. The museum is dedicated to the country and western singer-songwriter's legacy and contributions to country music — not only in his home province, but the world — and shares Snow's fascinating story for new generations. The museum is housed inside Liverpool's railroad station — a place where, as a boy, he sought shelter many nights from his abusive grandmother.

SEACAN STUDIO

When the Covid-19 pandemic hit in March 2020, followed by progressive lockdowns, Adrian Sutherland already knew isolation well. The front man and founder of the band Midnight Shine grew up — and still calls home — one of the most remote and isolated First Nation communities in Canada: Attawapiskat, located on James Bay, more than 500 kilometres north of Timmins, Ontario.

The pandemic pause allowed Sutherland time to reflect and to write. Stuck at home with no possible tour dates, the artist decided to make his first solo record. Grammy-winner Colin Linden produced and mixed the bulk of the songs remotely at his Nashville studio while Sutherland worked from his home in Attawapiskat First Nation. Getting the songs written was not a problem. The challenge was finding a space to record. Fortunately for the songwriter, resource-fulness is a requirement for living in the Far North. The songwriter decided to think "inside the box" and one day an idea struck him. Sutherland had come into possession of a 40-foot sea container a few years back and figured he could retrofit a section of it into a makeshift studio. There were some logistical obstacles, and it took two weeks to complete, but Sutherland got it done with the help of friends and neighbours. Dubbed the SeaCan Studio, Sutherland transformed the unit into a useable recording studio by installing drywall and wood panelling on the interior and getting a local electrician to install the wiring necessary for the lights, heat, and recording gear.

The resulting songs recorded remotely in SeaCan ended up on Sutherland's Juno-nominated solo debut *When the Magic Hits*, released September 17, 2021. The themes tackled on this album are more personal and sensitive than the artist's work with Midnight Shine.

TRAIL-BLAZING WANKERS FROM LONDON

Flash back to the late 1970s. London, Ontario, is sleepy, conservative. Punk rock it is not. Yet, after dark, if you know where to look, there is definitely a seedier — and more exciting — side to this southwestern Ontario city. When the nine-to-fivers go to bed, rock clubs like Fryfogle's come alive. This is where the first true punk event in the Forest City occurred when U.K. band Eddie and the Hot Rods played the venue in the fall of 1977. There is also a "loft scene" in the downtown core where artists, outcasts, and transients live and mingle.

In this environment, the punk band the Demics was formed. Their first official gig was at one of the aforementioned lofts on December 23, 1977, to 250 people. Keith Whittaker, one of the band's founders, christened the punk rock outfit with its name. "Demic" was a Manchester (where Whittaker immigrated from) slang insult that meant "loser" or "wanker." Joining Whittaker in the Demics were Jimmy Weatherstone, Iain Atkinson-Staines, and Rob Brent. Word of mouth led the owner of the York Hotel — a watering hole where Whittaker liked to hang his hat and have a few — to hire them as a house band, due to the size of their audience and their insatiable love of libations.

The band outgrew the London scene and moved to Toronto to be in the middle of Canada's biggest punk scene, where bands like the Viletones were popular. The Demics figured they had a better chance to see and be seen and land a record deal in the big city. In 1979, Steve Koch, who had quit the Viletones that December, met and befriended Whittaker, a busboy by day at the Horseshoe Tavern, and joined the punk outfit when Rob Brent left. The Viletones' guitarist Freddy Pompeii got the Demics their first Toronto gig — an opening slot for Pompeii's band at "the Shoe."

"New York City" — from their debut EP *Talk's Cheap*, released on Ready Records — was a hit on CFNY in 1979. Since then the song has perennially ranked high in many best-of lists of the greatest Canadian singles of all time. Though the band broke up after only two records, the Demics were a fan favourite that never got its due. In retrospect, they were an influential part of the first wave of punk rock and new wave in Canada.

BUBBLEGUM POP OR RAGE-RIDDEN ROCK?

Before she was that "Ironic" girl, Alanis Morissette was a TV star and teenage pop princess. At 14 years old, Morissette signed with MCA Records after the label saw her sing on the children's TV show *You Can't Do That on Television*. The label wanted to groom her to be a Canadian version of Debbie Gibson or Tiffany.

Morissette recorded a pair of Canadian-release-only albums: *Alanis* in 1991, and *Now Is the Time* in 1992. The self-titled debut dance/pop record sold 200,000 copies and featured the Top 10 single "Too Hot."

Flash forward a few years. The "pop princess" had moved to Los Angeles looking for a change in sound and style. Morissette was 20 years old when she wrote the songs for *Jagged Little Pill*, her angst alternative-rock album that struck a chord in the late 1990s. Nearly every major record label passed on this collection of songs. Eventually, Maverick Records — the label co-founded by Madonna — signed Morissette. Other than "Ironic," which Alanis co-wrote with producer Glen Ballard (Michael Jackson, Wilson Phillips), the rest of the lyrics came directly from the songwriter's diary.

Released June 13, 1995, the record sold 10 million copies in its first year and went to number one in 13 countries. The Canadian made the cover of *Rolling Stone* that year with a headline that read: "Angry White Female." Since its release, *Jagged Little Pill* has added another 20 million in sales — making it one of the bestselling albums of all time. The record was nominated for nine Grammy Awards and won four. At the time, the 21-year-old was the youngest artist to win Album of the Year. Another milestone for Alanis and this record: she was the first Canadian to achieve double diamond status for sales of more than two million.

NOVA SCOTIA'S "GIFT FROM HEAVEN"

Born in Truro, Nova Scotia, in 1911, Portia White (whose name was inspired by the heroine in Shakespeare's *The Merchant of Venice*) had a dream to become a professional singer. The third of 13 children born to William and Izie Dora White, she started singing in the church choir at six years old. With hard work, discipline, and determination (walking 15 kilometres a week for music lessons) the contralto made this dream a reality — becoming the first Black Canadian concert singer to make a name for herself on the international stage. This fact is not surprising when you learn White came from a family of trailblazers who did not let their skin colour become a barrier to success despite living in a period of widespread discrimination. White's father, the minister of the local Baptist Church, was the second

Black Canadian to be admitted to Acadia University and became the first Black Canadian to receive a Ph.D., earning a Doctorate of Divinity from this post-secondary institution.

A stroke of luck also played a role in White's success. In 1938, the renowned baritone Ernesto Vinci (born Ernst Wreszynski in Gnesen, Prussia) arrived in Halifax via New York. He was hired as the new director for the Conservatory of Music in Halifax. The Halifax Ladies' Musical Club awarded Portia a scholarship to study under Vinci, who trained her in the famed bel canto method. White made her formal debut at the Eaton Auditorium in Toronto on November 7, 1941. Edward Wodson, reviewing the show, wrote that White's voice was a "gift from heaven."

Later, she performed at New York's Town Hall on March 13, 1944 — becoming the first Canadian to perform at the venue. In 1945, the Canadian contralto signed with Columbia Concerts. In the years that followed, she toured North, Central, and South America. After a life on the road became too tiring, White gave back to other aspiring soloists by offering the gift of her voice to other students, both giving private lessons and teaching at Toronto's Branksome Hall.

In 1995, the Government of Canada named White "a person of national significance." Today a commemorative plaque is located outside the Zion United Baptist Church in her hometown, along with a life-size sculpture of White carved out of a tree.

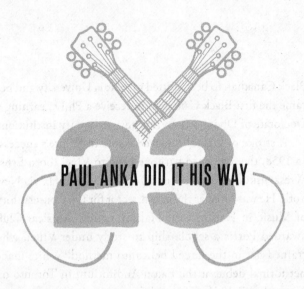

23

PAUL ANKA DID IT HIS WAY

Long before the teenage heartthrob known as the Biebs, there was an Ottawa boy with drive and determination who wrote hit song after hit song.

At 13 years old, Paul Anka had already assembled his first vocal group, the Bobby Soxers. At 15, he travelled to Manhattan and used some sweet-talking to get a meeting with A&R representative Don Costa at ABC-Paramount Records. Anka played him "Diana." Costa heard something in the song, and it became Anka's first number one hit.

Anka also penned the timeless classic "My Way," written for Frank Sinatra but covered by countless artists from Elvis Presley to the Sex Pistols' Sid Vicious. Here's how it was born.

At 16 years old, after Top 10 singles including "Lonely Boy," "Put Your Head on My Shoulder," and "Puppy Love,"

Anka was hired to headline the Sands Hotel and Casino in Las Vegas where he met Sinatra, who mentored the teenage star. The seeds for "My Way" began during a dinner Anka had with Sinatra in Miami where Old Blue Eyes told the Canadian he was retiring. Anka felt an urge that night to write a song that paid homage to his friend and mentor.

Back home in New York City, Anka got to work. First, he set lyrics to the music of the 1967 French song "Comme d'habitude" by Claude François, Jacques Revaux, and Gilles Thibaut, which he had first heard while on vacation in the south of France. Anka bought the rights to this song and as he looked to rework the melody and rewrite the lyrics, he channelled Sinatra and tried to write the song in his hero's voice. What might the master speak? What words would he use to express his life in song? A writing session with his IBM typewriter began shortly after midnight. With thunder booming outside his apartment, Anka blocked out Mother Nature's noise and hammered at the keys. By 5 a.m. he had written "My Way."

Anka flew to Vegas the next day and played the song for Sinatra, who loved it and quickly recorded it in one take — releasing the song in 1969. It peaked at No. 27 on the Billboard Hot 100 and spent a record 124 weeks on the U.K. singles chart, reaching fifth spot. In 2008, the song was inducted into the Canadian Songwriters Hall of Fame.

CANADA'S POLKA KING

More than 50 albums, a member of both the
Order of Canada and Canada's Walk of Fame, along
with three Grammy Awards ... not a bad resumé for a
polka artist. Born in Duparquet, Quebec, in 1935, Walter
Ostanek started playing the piano accordion as a boy and
mastered the instrument before he turned 12. Influenced
by his Yugoslavian parents and the American polka phe-
nom Frank Yankovic, Ostanek fell in love with Slovenian-
style polka. In 1957, at 16 years old, he formed his first
group, the Walter Ostanek Band. They quickly became
a fixture at Oktoberfest events throughout Canada and
the United States — especially in Kitchener-Waterloo,
Ontario, which boasts the largest annual German festival
outside of Munich.

Ostanek's Polka King title is well deserved. He hosted the variety show *Polka Time* for 24 years and has even performed at Nashville's music shrine, the Grand Ole Opry. For more than 70 years, Ostanek and his band have led revellers at festival halls across North America in doing the bird dance and singing German drinking songs such as "Ein Prosit" and "In Heaven There Is No Beer." When not performing, the Polka King owned and operated a retail store (Ostanek's Music Centre) in his adopted hometown of St. Catharines before selling the space to Long & McQuade. In 2016, Ostanek won the $1 million grand prize in London, Ontario's Dream Lottery. A sad fact that breaks Ostanek's heart is that there is no longer a golden gramophone to win for future purveyors of polka since the Recording Academy (the administrator of the Grammys) did away with the Best Polka Album category in 2009.

"BEATLEMANIA" COINED BY A CANADIAN

An Ottawa reporter took credit for coining the phrase "Beatlemania" to describe the pandemonium that swept through Britain and arrived in North America in the early 1960s. The journalist's name? Sandy Gardiner — who wrote for the *Ottawa Journal* in the nation's capital.

The music reporter started his career in England in the early 1960s and moved to Canada in 1962, finding employment at the *Journal*. Gardiner had a weekly music column that was published in the Saturday edition of the paper called Platter, Patter … and Idol Chatter. In his November 9, 1963, column, Gardiner wrote a "new disease is sweeping through Britain, Europe and the Far East" that "doctors are powerless to stop. The name of this new addition to the world of Ben Casey's and Doc Kildare's is — BEATLEMANIA."

Beatles scholars later revealed the term was published in U.K. tabloid the *Daily Mirror* a few weeks before, which, in the days before the internet, most likely Gardiner had not read, to describe a riot by fans following a Beatles performance on October 14, 1963.

Still, Gardiner's usage is historic and worth noting as it caught on in the lexicon following his penning the word in his column to mean the fan pandemonium. The Fab Four's debut Canadian release of *Meet the Beatles*, called *Beatlemania! With the Beatles*, included Gardiner's quote on the cover.

THE MAHARAJA OF THE KEYBOARD

A Canadian jazz legend and winner of eight Grammy Awards, pianist Oscar Peterson won a CBC national contest at age 14 after his sister persuaded him to audition. This set him on the road to success, and he became a regular on the CBC show *The Happy Gang*. Peterson's father, a porter with the Canadian Pacific Railway, was a self-taught piano player and passed on his gift to Oscar.

Oscar's big break came in 1959 when Norman Granz, producer of the popular Jazz at the Philharmonic shows, which played regularly at venues across North America, heard one of Peterson's songs broadcast live from the Alberta Lounge on the car radio on his way to the Montreal airport. Granz figured his flight could wait; he had to meet this talent immediately. The American record producer told the taxi driver to take him directly to the venue. From this initial meeting, Granz gave Peterson a chance to perform as a surprise guest at Carnegie Hall and become a permanent member of the Jazz at the Philharmonic touring band. During his career, Peterson played with such jazz legends as Ella Fitzgerald, Dizzy Gillespie, and Charlie Parker. American jazz great Duke Ellington even called Peterson "the Maharaja of the Keyboard."

RISE OF THE POOL SINGER

Born in Detroit, Michigan, Liberty Silver was adopted by a Canadian family as a toddler and moved to Peterborough, Ontario. Before all her awards and accolades, Silver's first paying gig came at the age of 12 when she found herself in a reggae band opening for Bob Marley (who she did not even know) in New York City at Madison Square Garden.

How did this opening slot come about? Pure luck. A young Silver was visiting her older sister in Toronto and started singing as she swam in the pool. This caught the ear of a stranger passing through, who was drawn to her soulful voice. The stranger turned out to be a music promoter. An audition was arranged, and the next thing she knew, Silver was on a bus heading to New York City to open for Marley.

In the mid-'80s Liberty Silver took the music industry by storm, racking up five Juno nominations and two wins between 1985 and 1989, earning her a place in history as the first Black woman to win a Juno Award, as well as the first-ever recipient of the Best R&B/Soul Recording of the Year for her single "Lost Somewhere Inside Your Love."

In 1985, on "Tears Are Not Enough" — the charity song written and recorded to raise money and awareness for the famine in Ethiopia — Silver sang a verse with Loverboy's Mike Reno. The artist also co-wrote and performed the official theme songs at the Olympic Games in 1996 and 2004.

CANADA'S MUSIC PRODIGY

David Foster was born in Victoria, British Columbia.
The son of a blue-collar worker and a homemaker, Foster
started playing — and studying — piano at age four. One
morning his mom was dusting the family piano when she
hit a key by accident and David said, "That's an E!" naming
the correct note.

By age 13, Foster was studying music at the University of
Washington. When the family moved to Edmonton, Alberta,
the teenager led a nightclub band in a joint owned by jazz
piano player and arranger Tommy Banks. The impresario
took Foster under his wing and encouraged the young music
prodigy to write. Thanks to Banks's tutelage on the art of ar-
ranging — and the hard work of gigging in bands throughout
the early to mid-1970s — Foster's songs kept getting better.

As a keyboardist during this early chapter of his career, Foster played on a pair of George Harrison records (*Extra Texture* and *Thirty Three & 1/3*) and also lent over-dubbed piano to Lynyrd Skynyrd's third studio album, *Nuthin' Fancy*. One of his early production credits was Alice Cooper's fourth solo studio record, *From the Inside*, which chronicled Cooper's time inside a New York sanatorium during a rehab stint for alcoholism.

David Foster is now one of the biggest names in the music business. He has written songs for Whitney Houston, Chicago, Kanye West, Celine Dion, and Drake, as well as serving as chair for Verve Records, and has racked up 16 Grammys, an Emmy, a Golden Globe, and three Oscar nominations.

WRESTLING AGAINST RACISM

If you grew up in the 1960s, hearing the name the Rascals brings earworms of the New Jersey soul group, often called the Young Rascals, that featured Canadian guitarist Gene Cornish and had a string of Billboard No. 1 hits. But add a Canadian "zed" instead of an "ess" at the end and you arrive at another pioneering band.

The Rascalz, formed in 1991, were one of the earliest hip-hop bands from Vancouver, British Columbia. The group popularized the term "Van City" and led the West Coast scene in the '90s. The Rascalz were also diehard wrestling fans and especially loved Canadian Bret "Hitman" Hart — a five-time WWF World Heavyweight Champion. Their song "Sharpshooter (Best of the Best)" was written for Hart to use as his theme song as he entered the arena and walked toward the ring. The title referred to the wrestler's signature finishing move, and the song sampled the Hitman's catch-phrase: "I am the best there is, the best there was, and the best there ever will be."

In 1993, Sony Music released a reworked version of their independent album, *Really Livin'*, which was nominated for a Juno Award in 1994 and 1995. In 1997 they moved to BMG Canada and released *Cash Crop*, which was certified gold, selling more than 50,000 copies in Canada. The al-bum was nominated for a Juno in 1998 in the Best Rap Recording category and won. The Rascalz declined the award, claiming racism because the award had little visibil-ity and was not awarded as part of the main ceremony.

The band issued the following statement: "In view of the lack of real inclusion of Black music in this ceremony, this feels like a token gesture toward honoring the real impact of urban music in Canada. Urban music, reggae, R&B, and rap, that's all Black music, and it's not represented [at the Junos]. We decided that until it is, we were going to take a stance." The band inspired a whole generation of future Canadian hip-hop artists, such as k-os, who says that with-out the early support of this pioneering hip-hop group, he would not have a career.

One final fascinating fact about *Cash Crop*: the record's biggest track "Northern Touch" was not even included on the original pressing. The song, which featured Checkmate,

Kardinal Offishall, Thrust, and Choclair, was released as a non-album single in 1998 and ended up becoming one of the biggest hits in Canadian hip-hop history.

MAPLE MUSIC JUNKET

The myth that you had to make it in the United States to validate your talent because Canada did not have a true and supportive industry started in the 1960s. Neil Young, frustrated by his slow march to success in his home country, bought a hearse and headed to L.A. The rest is history. Joni Mitchell followed a similar path, achieving her California dreams.

At the time, Europeans were more aware of acts south of our border and lumped Canadian artists in with those from the U.S. In the early 1970s, the music press in the U.K. did not know the variety of unique songwriters and groups that were emerging in Canada and that indeed we had our own scene, and the talent pool ran deep. Even some of our most successful artists, such as the Guess Who and Gordon

Lightfoot, many presses across the pond thought were just North American music. This story is about how a pair of Canadians sought to change that narrative.

In 1972, music journalist Ritchie Yorke and Capitol Records Canada president Arnold Gosewich invited about 80 European record producers and reporters to Canada for an all-expenses-paid, four-day trip to experience the Canadian music scene. CP Air chartered this distinguished group to Canada. The pair were aided by representatives from more than a dozen other record companies. This junket in early June featured concerts first in Montreal followed by a pair of back-to-back shows in Toronto at Massey Hall. For the artists who played these gigs, it was definitely a boost for the better.

"This event was about trying to get us in the position where a Valdy, or any one of these Canadian musicians, could be a musician who doesn't rely on being a cover band," says Bill King, who was part of the junket lineup, backing up singer-songwriter Chris Kearney at Massey Hall.

On June 7, Crowbar capped off the evening and the junket. The band knew they had to make a statement. The visiting journalists were worn out from the whirlwind trip. As Crowbar's drummer Sonnie Bernardi reflected years later: "We really had to do something to catch these fellas and entertain them. We are downhill skiing with no poles!"

What an entrance the band made. Crowbar were brought on by six pipers playing "Amazing Grace." The stage came alive with lights, smoke, and a huge cardboard cake. Before they even started to play, a topless woman emerged from the cake, followed by the band members. Larger-than-life lead singer Kelly Jay was the last to appear, opening bottles of champagne, sharing it with those in the front row and spraying others in the audience. A high-energy set followed. Not a soul in the theatre remained in their seats. All were standing, clapping, hooting, and hollering. Bernardi believes Crowbar's stellar performance helped the band get the slots and venues they did when they finally toured in Europe.

Crowbar was not the only act that benefitted from the junket. It left a lasting impression on the Europeans. Archival interview footage with one of the visiting reporters attests to the Maple Music Junket's success: "I thought Canadian music is the same like American music, but now I know the difference."

THE GREATEST "UNKNOWN" GUITARIST

Lenny Breau was a fingerstyle jazz player un-known to many music fans until after his death, but well-known among musicians who tried to emulate — and learn from — his style. Breau was born in Maine, but moved with his family to the Maritimes when he was just seven years old. Around age 11, Breau picked up the guitar for the first time after hearing a Chet Atkins instrumental on the radio. He was in awe of how Atkins got the instrument's sound and tried to copy the guitarist's unique thumb pick and fingerstyle technique.

Breau's earliest stage appearances came with his parents, who performed as the country and western duo Hal "Lone Pine" Breau and yodeller Betty Cody (born Rita Coté). Lenny's stage name was Lone Pine Junior. The family moved to Winnipeg in 1957, where the couple hosted a daily radio show called *Caravan* on the local station CKY. During his teenage years, Lenny became fascinated with jazz and fell into the local music scene. His influences in this period of self-taught education were jazz pianist Bill Evans (Breau picked up on his complicated harmonics and melodic concepts) and flamenco guitarists.

A meeting with a young Randy Bachman occurred around this time, with Breau giving Bachman some lessons. The future songwriter and guitarist in the Guess Who and Bachman-Turner Overdrive became a lifelong fan of Breau's.

Chet Atkins, who recorded Breau's solo debut, *Guitar Sounds from Lenny Breau,* in 1968, when he was vice-president of RCA Records, called him "the greatest guitar player ever." A little-known fact: Breau briefly toured in 1972 as a member of Anne Murray's band but was fired due to his growing drug use and its effect on his performances.

On August 12, 1984, Breau was found murdered in the rooftop swimming pool of his L.A. apartment. He was only 43 years old. Although his third wife, Jewel Glasscock, was a suspect, there was not enough evidence to bring charges against her, so no one was ever charged with the crime. Breau was buried in an unmarked grave in Forest Lawn cemetery in L.A. A tragic end for an unsung Canadian guitar virtuoso.

HI-FI BOOM & BUST

Did you know a pair of Canadian university students designed and sold one of the world's strangest — and most expensive — stereos? The Clairtone cost as much as a small car when it was launched in the late 1950s. The hi-fi system was the brainchild of Toronto entrepreneurs Peter Munk (who later founded Barrick Gold, the world's largest gold mining operation) and David Gilmour.

Munk and Gilmour's innovative idea was to build a high-end stereo that doubled as a fashionable piece of furniture inspired by the trendy Scandinavian designs that were popular at the time. But building these masterpiece machines handcrafted with Canadian timber bled cash, and the two founders had to mortgage their homes to keep the company going before taking the firm public in 1960.

Sales went from $642,000 in 1959 (its first full year of operation) to $11 million in 1965. During its peak in popularity, Simpsons at Queen and Yonge in downtown Toronto reported selling one unit every three hours.

Celebrities endorsed the high-end product and conversation piece in people's homes. Frank Sinatra owned one, so did *Playboy* founder Hugh Hefner. The Project G model, with a price tag of up to $1,850, featured space-age styling and a pair of black, globelike speakers. Masters at marketing, Clairtone targeted both men and women, and the hi-fi product was also placed in many movies. Rewatch classics like *The Graduate* or Sinatra's romantic comedy *Marriage on the Rocks* today and you can spot one of these Swinging Sixties status symbols.

The company ended up building a plant in Stellarton, Nova Scotia, on a seven-acre property. The plant brought hundreds of jobs and gave a boost to the local economy. Those on the assembly lines produced 20 different models of the Clairtone and 60 percent of these front-line workers were women.

By 1970, production of Clairtone's hi-fi stereos stopped. One mistake was adding a line of televisions. Add in union problems at the Nova Scotia plant, and Clairtone had run its course and shut its doors. No matter, Munk's first company remains a piece of Canadian music history. And, as recently as 2021, some Clairtone models have become collectibles again with professional basketball star LeBron James adding one to his "crib."

SISTINE CHAPEL OF ROCK 'N' ROLL

Did you know the National Music Centre in Calgary owns a piece of rock 'n' roll history where classic rock anthems like Led Zeppelin's "Stairway to Heaven," the Rolling Stones' "Brown Sugar," and Deep Purple's "Smoke on the Water" were recorded?

The Rolling Stones Mobile (RSM) is a state-of-the-art recording studio, equipped with a Helios console, that is mounted on a truck. Built in 1968, it was revolutionary technology that allowed artists to make and record music anywhere and at any time. The innovative studio on wheels was the brainchild of Rolling Stones tour manager Ian Stewart. The Stones used it and also rented it out to other musicians. Some of the biggest records of the 1970s were made using the RSM, including *Alchemy: Dire Straits Live*, *Machine Head* (Deep Purple), and *Led Zeppelin IV*.

The National Music Centre purchased the historic RSM for Studio Bell in 2001. Their electronics technician, John Leimseider, restored what he called the "Sistine Chapel of rock 'n' roll" in 2015. Today, it's not only a permanent exhibit open to the public, but artists who make a record at Studio Bell can use the RSM.

HIP-HOP FREEDOM

It's 1991. You are 13 years old. Civil war and extreme violence are all you know. You live in war-torn Somalia and your family narrowly escapes death getting on one of the last flights out of the country to start a new life as refugees in North America.

That's Canadian-Somalian hip-hop artist K'Naan's story in a nutshell. The artist rose to fame in 2010 when "Wavin' Flag," from his album *Troubadour*, became an anthem for freedom thanks to Coca-Cola picking it as the official theme song for the 2010 FIFA World Cup. That same year, a remake of the song featuring an all-star cast of Canadian musicians was recorded under the name Young Artists for Haiti to raise money for the island nation following a devastating earthquake.

It's not like the refugee life was perfect for the young aspiring poet and songwriter. The family's first stop was New York. There, K'Naan survived the ghettoes and gangs of Harlem before they moved to the Toronto neighbourhood of Rexdale. K'Naan (born Keinan, which means "traveller" in Somalian) was also picked on by schoolmates upon arrival to Canada. Words and music helped him cope. Perhaps it was the lines from the song — about becoming stronger with age and embodying freedom — which were passed on to him by his grandfather, a famous Somalian poet, that inspired him the most.

35

WHAT THE TRUCK?

A studio on wheels where magic musical moments happened and Grammy-winning songs were captured to tape. That was the Enactron Truck — one of the first-ever mobile recording units. It was the brainchild of Canadian award-winning record producer Brian Ahern, who converted a semi-trailer into a mobile recording studio.

A "control room on wheels," the 42-foot-long unit allowed artists to record whenever — and wherever — they wanted. The idea came to the musician in the early 1970s while living in Toronto.

The first three shows Ahern (who was born in Halifax) recorded with the truck were performed by the string section of the Toronto Symphony Orchestra at Massey Hall. In 1974, Ahern, like many Canadian artists during that time, packed up his belongings and truck and moved to California — setting it up on the lot of a Hollywood mansion he rented in Beverly Hills on Lania Lane, just off Mulholland Drive.

Once in Los Angeles, the Enactron Truck was in regular use. In 1976, the mobile studio was used to record *The Last Waltz* (the final concert by the Band) and *A Star Is Born* with Barbra Streisand. Other artists to record with this unique studio included Dolly Parton, Willie Nelson, Kris Kristofferson, Bob Dylan, and Black Sabbath. Many TV shows and films also used the truck to make final mixes to their soundtracks.

In her memoir *Composed*, Rosanne Cash wrote that working in the Enactron Truck was like being in a submarine. Today, the innovative studio is no longer in use, but is preserved at the Musicians Hall of Fame and Museum in Nashville, Tennessee, where plans are underway to make this piece of music history a permanent exhibit.

36

A LESSON FOR OPENERS

"Don't upstage them!" These are the simple
three words of advice Great Big Sea's Séan McCann gives
any band that gets an opening slot for a bigger, more established group.

In 1995, Great Big Sea had just released their Warner
Music Canada debut *Up*. And, like the title suggests, the
Newfoundland Celtic-rock band were on the rise. Since
Spirit of the West and Great Big Sea shared a record label,
their managers thought pairing these groups for a cross-
Canada tour was a good match. Apparently, it was *too* good.

"We were rising, coming up behind them, and they were
aware of us," McCann recalls of this opening slot. "We were
supposed to do thirty dates and they kicked us off after only
six! We were coming out to kill them every night. They were

so nice about it, and apologetic when they told us, but they simply said, 'guys, we love you, but we are going to go with the Philosopher Kings because they are not like us and they are not like you!'"

Before Spirit of the West's lead singer John Mann got sick with Alzheimer's, the bands toured together again and they got payback.

"They opened for us and did the same thing," McCann says. "They tried to smoke us every night and some nights they did! It's a real tightrope you are walking as an opener. You got to win the day without smoking the main act because, as we found out, they will kick you off!"

THE MONTREAL BED-IN

A piece of Canadian music history happened on May 26, 1969, when John Lennon and his new bride Yoko Ono (the celebrity couple had married just two months before in Gibraltar) camped out for one week in room 1742, and the adjoining rooms 1738, 1740, and 1744, at the Queen Elizabeth hotel in Montreal in protest against war. With them was Ono's five-year-old daughter, Kyoko.

The hippie couple's sojourn in La Belle Province lasted eight days and was part of a bed-in for world peace campaign that began in Amsterdam and continued in the Bahamas before touching down in Montreal. Their visit drew not just fans, but also friends and fellow celebrities, who came to support the cause and to just hang, like British Grammy-winning songwriter Petula Clark ("Downtown"), beat poet

Allen Ginsberg, and counterculture hero and LSD advocate Timothy Leary.

While people came and went around them, John and Oko remained in bed, dressed in matching white pyjamas, holding hands. The room was decorated with white chrysanthemums and carnations, record players, and film equipment.

This giant slumber party in these hotel suites also birthed one of the world's most famous anti-war anthems: "Give Peace a Chance." As Lennon lay in bed strumming his 1964 Gibson, everyone in the room sang along and Montreal sound engineer André Perry recorded the impromptu session live in the hotel suite late one night. On July 7, the single was released and peaked at No. 14 on the Billboard charts. Today, the Bed-In Suite at that historic hotel (now owned by Fairmont) is a tourist attraction.

38 TRANSCRIBING A "TAUPIN" POP HIT

Jane Harbury, born in the U.K., arrived in Toronto in 1966 looking for adventure with a one-year plan. She never left. More than a half-century later the adventures continue for the affable Harbury, who fell into the music industry. Stories from her years working as a publicist and promoter could fill a book.

Here's a tale she shared about the time in the 1970s when she was working as a receptionist at Eastern Sound Studio — the famed pair of Victorian houses at 48 Yorkville Avenue in Toronto (now a luxury high-rise condo) where everyone from Canadians Bruce Cockburn, Anne Murray, Murray McLauchlan, and Gordon Lightfoot ("Sundown" was recorded in these four walls) to international stars like Elton John and Bruce Springsteen made magic.

In March 1976, Elton John and producer Gus Dudgeon had taken over Eastern Sound. Along with John's band, the musicians lived in Yorkville for nearly six weeks, staying at the nearby Park Hyatt. What came out of these sessions was John's 11th studio record — the double album *Blue Moves*, which peaked at No. 3 on the U.S. Billboard charts.

Local chauffeur John Cunningham called Harbury from his presidential Lincoln limousine each morning to announce Elton's arrival. Fans of the British pop-rock star gathered outside the studio hoping to catch a glimpse of John before he darted into the studio. On March 25, John even celebrated his 29th birthday during these Eastern Sound sessions. At Harbury's encouragement (she had heard his admirers serenading him outside the studio) John was persuaded to take a short break and acknowledge the crowd. Elton came outside and conducted his delirious fans in a rousing rendition of "Happy Birthday."

A couple of days after his birthday, John came out of the studio to give Harbury a message. It's a day she's never forgotten. The songwriter asked her if Bernie Taupin, his partner in song, had called. Harbury replied that he had not. John then told her that he was waiting for Taupin (who was down in Barbados) to call with the lyrics to the band's first planned single.

Maybe an hour or so later Taupin called and Harbury transcribed the lyrics he dictated. She excitedly ran into the studio to give them to John. The song was "Don't Go Breaking My Heart." It was not released on *Blue Moves* but was a stand-alone single that ended up spending four weeks at No. 1 on the Billboard charts.

PRINCE OF BLUES ON BELLAIR

By the 2000s, the folk-hippie mecca of Toronto's Yorkville neighbourhood had become better known for its Gucci purses, art galleries, wine bars, and luxury boutiques. Amidst this glitz and glam, John Daly, whose day job was editor at the *Globe and Mail*, was playing rhythm guitar in a bar band backing local harmonica player Jerome Godboo. Two sets are nearly done at Blues on Bellair when a muscular guy entered the bar and asked if Prince could sit in with the band and borrow Daly's Gibson Les Paul Classic six-string electric.

Minutes later, Prince sauntered in with his Canadian wife, Manuela Testolini. The artist had recently bought a home in the tony Bridle Path neighbourhood in North Toronto and had popped in unannounced at several recent events. Still, it was a surprise sighting for a Saturday night. Prince sported a powder blue suit with matching blue suede boots. He picked up Daly's axe, letting the strap fall to the floor, and sat on the guitarist's amplifier. Prince jammed with the band on a 12-bar blues to end the second set.

During the break, the Grammy-winning artist chatted with the band's bassist — Prakash John, a local legend and part of the original "Toronto sound," who had played with Lou Reed and Alice Cooper. Prince rejoined the band in the evening's final set, borrowing Daly's Gibson again, and showcasing his skills by cranking up the wah-wah and distortion for "a '70s-style epic" that meandered along for 10 minutes. When the song ended, Prince handed the guitar back to the journalist. Thankfully, despite the workout, no strings had broken. Prakash's son Jordan, 16 years old at the time and manning the drums that night, exclaimed: "Well, that's it. I'm retiring!"

THE LOST HEATWAVE TAPES

The Kings formed in Oakville in 1977 and built-up a following gig by gig playing Ontario bars from east to west and north to south. Their biggest hit, "This Beat Goes On/Switchin' to Glide," was inducted into the Canadian Songwriters Hall of Fame in 2020. One-hit wonders to some, the band has remained together and been making original music for more than 40 years. The Kings performed on Dick Clark's *American Bandstand* and toured across North America opening for big rock acts like Bob Seger, Jeff Beck, Eric Clapton, and the Beach Boys.

For the band, who still tours today and continues to make new music, one of the highlights was headlining the Heatwave Festival on August 23, 1980, at Mosport Park. Their debut, *The Kings Are Here*, was released that same year. Heatwave saw more than 50,000 people gather for a new wave/punk festival at Mosport raceway north of Bowmanville, Ontario. The lineup featured the B-52's, Elvis Costello, the Pretenders, and Talking Heads. The Clash were originally announced as headliners — and listed on promotional posters — but never showed. Canadians on the bill, beside the Kings, included Teenage Head. Tickets were only $20. The Kings were a relatively unknown band compared to other artists on the bill (their debut with the smash single "This Beat Goes On/Switchin' to Glide" had yet to be released); yet, they had the honour of closing the show thanks to their friendship with John Brower, the Toronto impresario who put the festival together. This gig led to much bigger stages for the Kings.

And thankfully, years later, they are one of the few bands that performed at Heatwave who have festival footage. A movie crew was there to shoot all the bands, but the Kings and Teenage Head were the only two to sign waivers giving the crew permission to film them. Band member Mister Zero reflects on this detail: "It's a pity because it could have been a Woodstock movie for the new wave and punk bands of the 1980s."

Canadian engineer Doug McClement recorded the audio in his mobile truck, but the video tapes from the Kings performance ended up in a vault and on a shelf somewhere and were not seen for more than a decade. A few years ago,

Mister Zero did some detective work and found the film production company that was hired to shoot the event. He called them up and when he explained what he was looking for, the guy on the other end of the line said he was lucky as they had recently done a purge of their tapes and the Heatwave one had survived. The band got the audio from McClement and matched it with the original video footage using the latest technology for cleaning up 16 mm film stock frame by frame.

41

KEY TO HELLO CITY

In 1991, Scarborough's Barenaked Ladies (BNL) were scheduled to perform to ring in the new year. Instead, the City of Toronto took offence to their name — banning them from performing at any city-sponsored event on the grounds that their name "objectified women." The ensuing national media story just helped bring notoriety for their music across Canada. A *Toronto Star* editorial ran on January 8, 1991, with the headline "Barenaked stupidity" and slammed the politicians for their nearsightedness. For their part, BNL ended up playing that New Year's Eve in Hamilton instead.

The band was gaining popularity already thanks to their self-titled five-track EP cassette, known as "the Yellow Tape" due to the colour of its cover, which featured the songs "Be My Yoko Ono," "Brian Wilson" and "If I Had a $1,000,000." Thanks to the publicity gained from the New Year's Eve ban, BNL went from selling 400 indie cassettes a week to 14,000 overnight — eventually selling more than 100,000 copies to become the first independent release to be certified platinum in Canada.

In April 1992, they signed a worldwide deal with New York–based Sire Records. Their major-label debut, *Gordon*, released that July, has been certified diamond — selling more than one million copies in Canada. So it was a wee bit ironic when, in 1994, Mayor June Rowlands, who had felt the band's name objectified women, wanted to give the key to the city to the band to honour their commercial success. BNL refused, not wanting to get involved in local politics and remembering the earlier snub.

The genesis for the band's name actually came when band members Ed Robertson and Steven Page were bored at a Bob Dylan concert and just started to make up fake band names to pass the time — one of the names included before settling on Barenaked Ladies was "Pierre Berton's Pants." One can only speculate as to how Toronto city council would have reacted to that one.

42

JEFF HEALEY'S LEGENDARY RECORD COLLECTION

Jeff Healey was a Grammy Award–winning musician, one-time bar owner, and one of Canada's most renowned blues guitarists. He was known for his innovative style due to his blindness — playing his electric guitar on his lap like a slide guitar, which he learned how to do at the age of three after losing his vision because of retinoblastoma, a rare form of cancer that targets the eyes.

Healey's massive record collection was as legendary as the artist himself. At 27,000 vinyl, this was more than just a hobby for the musician. The collection included 78 RPMs all stacked on shelves he had built. The basement of his Toronto home was filled with vinyl from floor to ceiling: lots of jazz but also big band dance music from the '20s,

'30s, and '40s. When he was not playing or touring, Healey enjoyed spinning these vintage records on the radio as a DJ for CBC Radio and Jazz.FM.

The records did not have Braille lettering; nor were they protected like most collections in plastic sleeves. They were just packed together. Amazingly, Healey could find any record you asked for among this vast collection without being able to see the titles on the albums.

MUCH ADO ABOUT MUCH

43

"MuchMusic. It was like electricity being created. It was that powerful ... it saved careers. It created careers; it was everything." This quote comes from Loverboy's Mike Reno in Christopher Ward's book *Is This Live? Inside the Wild Early Years of MuchMusic: The Nation's Music Station*, and captures the significance of the station that made TV stars out of Canadian musicians and helped launch the careers of many artists — especially in the channel's early days in the mid- to late 1980s.

Launched on August 31, 1984, as a pay-TV channel, by 1989 MuchMusic was added to regular cable service. The 24-hour music channel was the first in Canada dedicated entirely to music programming, following on the heels of MTV from south of the border just three years after that channel was born. The voice-over launching MuchMusic's debut proclaimed: "The best in music videos from ABC to ZZ Top, all for less than the cost of a burger and fries."

An opening reception for the public and industry at CITY-TV's Queen Street East studios saw more than 1,000 show up for the celebrations. Artists at the launch party included Platinum Blonde, Triumph, Kim Mitchell, Geddy Lee, and the Spoons. The first music video shown was for Rush's "The Enemy Within" — a single from their *Grace Under Pressure* album. While MuchMusic studios were originally located in a former dance club called Electric Circus, it later moved into 299 Queen Street West and became a beacon in the arts scene of the Queen Street West strip.

With the new channel also came a new noun into the lexicon — VJs, short for Video Jockeys. Anything was possible and improvisation was encouraged. As former MuchMusic VJ Erica Ehm called working there, it was a time of "beautiful chaos" that was often unscripted and off the wall. The VJs became celebrities in their own right and could often be spotted on Queen West, such as Mike & Mike (Mike Campbell and Mike Rhodes), whose *Mike and Mike's Excellent X-Canada Adventures* show ran on Much from 1986 for more than six years. The pair even had their own martini glasses at the nearby Horseshoe Tavern since that was their libation of choice and they were regulars at the front bar.

Speakers Corner, launched in 1990, was a video booth on Queen Street outside the station where, for a loonie, the public could record up to one-minute videos. The initial idea was a video version of Letters to the Editor, but the Barenaked Ladies changed that when they saw the platform's potential as a cheap marketing tool. In 1991, they crammed into the booth before one of their shows at the nearby Rivoli and sang a shortened version of "Be My Yoko Ono." Later, the booth was used to speak out on politics or show off your talents to the nation. The concept quickly caught on. By the late 1990s and early 2000s, there were Speakers Corner boxes in most of Canada's major cities.

While MuchMusic ceased broadcasting in 2001, it left a lasting legacy. For a generation of Canadian kids, before the internet, YouTube, and social media platforms like TikTok, this was the medium where music lovers discovered artists like Parachute Club, Blue Rodeo, Corey Hart, Platinum Blonde, the Pursuit of Happiness, Bryan Adams, Luba, and so many more.

SOCK IT TO ME

Musicians' backstage demands (usually referred to as hospitality riders) are further requests or additions to their concert contract — beyond playing at a specific date for a specific price and time. They run the gamut from the banal and usual fare of alcohol and food to the outrageous. One the most famous examples comes from Van Halen, who specified that "no brown-coloured M&Ms be allowed backstage at their concerts or the promoter would forfeit the entire show at full price." This ridiculous request was just a test — the band wanted to make sure the promoters actually read the contract.

Here's a fun story from a Canadian band about one of those unique contract requests. Vancouver alternative-rock four-piece the Grapes of Wrath had "four brand new pairs of men's dress socks" on its hospitality rider. This unusual demand came after the group shared a bill with the Jazz Butcher in 1988 and noticed they had this clause on their rider. "We thought it was a fantastic idea," recalls band member Kevin Kane. "Never again will we have to wear unclean socks whilst on tour!" Sometimes, however, promoters did not read the contract carefully enough and the band received athletic socks. Rather than forfeiting the gig, the band donated the socks to a member of their touring crew. Kane admits he gave away more pairs of socks than he kept.

Promoter Elliott Lefko gave guitarist Kane and his bandmates the most memorable pair of socks, which was apropos for the special nature of the gig — October 10, 1991, when the Grapes of Wrath headlined Massey Hall. The Grapes were the first band Lefko had ever promoted, making this milestone extra special. To mark the occasion, Elliott had custom knee-high socks made for each band member with fuzzy letters running the length of each sock spelling out each of their names.

45

NO SOPHOMORE SLUMP

This Child was Susan Aglukark's second album —
and it was definitely not the dreaded "sophomore slump"
that happens when a second album doesn't live up to the
hype of an artist's debut. Released on EMI in 1995, the record was Aglukark's commercial breakthrough in Canada —
spawning chart hits with "O Siem" and "Hina Na Ho
(Celebration)." The record sold more than 300,000 copies
(three times platinum) in Canada and peaked at No. 1 on
the Canadian RPM country charts. It was also nominated
for five awards at the 1996 Junos. With its success, Aglukark
became the first Inuk performer to earn a Juno Award and
have a Top 10 hit in Canada.

"We didn't expect a hit, it just happened," the songwriter
recalls. "'Nina Na Ho,' I had first heard with my previous

producer Randall Prescott just after the release of *Arctic Rose*. We tried something with this traditional Dene song. The person we credited with the writing was a Dene from Yellowknife. I tried a demo with Randall before bringing it to producer Chad [Irschick] during the *This Child* sessions."

On "O Siem" Aglukark sang in both Inuktitut and English; the song's uplifting tone carried a profound message from the artist's heart, calling out the need to eradicate racism and prejudice in our country. The line about being family resonated with Canadians, broke down barriers, and helped make this one of the most popular songs in 1995.

46
SARSSTOCK ROCKS

On July 30, 2003, the biggest concert before and since happened just north of Toronto at Downsview Park when close to 500,000 people came together in a fund-raising concert following the SARS outbreak that affected Toronto tourism. Officially called Molson Canadian Rocks for Toronto but dubbed "SARSstock" after the media picked up on the words a concertgoer had written across a large Canadian flag, it is one of the largest outdoor ticketed events ever held in Canadian history.

Earlier that year, the World Health Organization had issued a warning against non-essential travel to the city in the wake of the health crisis caused by SARS (Severe Acute Respiratory Syndrome) and the local economy took a hit. Toronto needed a PR boost to show the world it was once again safe to travel to Canada's largest city; what better way than to showcase this with a mammoth concert.

From the moment the gates to Downsview opened on the sweltering summer day, the fans flocked in and did not stop coming. The headliners to this 11-hour music marathon featuring 15 acts were no other than those kings of rock 'n' roll, the Rolling Stones.

Other international acts included AC/DC, Justin Timberlake, the Isley Brothers, and the Flaming Lips. For Timberlake, it was one of the artist's first solo appearances. Unfortunately, the rock 'n' roll crowd was not kind to the former NSYNC member — pelting Timberlake with bottles filled with urine. Seventeen years later, in an interview with CTV, the 10-time Grammy Award–winning artist said he still feels trauma when he recalls that day.

Rush, the Guess Who, Blue Rodeo, Kathleen Edwards, Sam Roberts, and the Tea Party supplied the Canadian content. Tickets were only $21.50, and Molson breweries signed on as one of the major sponsors — donating close to $5 million to help stage the event. The concert also raised funds for health-care and hospitality workers in the city, with the Stones agreeing to donate half of the net proceeds from any merchandise they sold, and one dollar from all tickets sold supporting front-line workers.

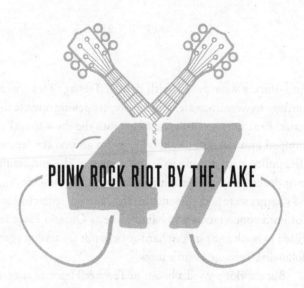

PUNK ROCK RIOT BY THE LAKE

Monday, June 2, 1980, is an infamous day in Toronto music history: Mayhem fuelled by teenage hormones and the punk-rock ethos of giving the middle finger to authority manifested itself by Lake Ontario. Here's what transpired.

Hamilton's favourite punk rockers, Teenage Head, were headlining a free show at the Ontario Place Forum, touring behind their album *Frantic City*. Management promoted the hell out of the show, and the group's manager even bused in fans. Their pavement pounding worked as more than 15,000 concertgoers showed up that June day on the shores of Lake Ontario. The problem — the venue could only accommodate a little over 10,000.

When police closed the gates, fans filled with rage fought back. Fences were torn down, police cars were overturned, and officers were pelted with debris. Teenage Head were onstage so were unaware of the melee happening outside the gates. Fans were so desperate to get into the show that they jumped into the lake and tried to swim around the fences. The police were waiting to scoop them up. The end result: two dozen people were injured, including 10 officers, and 58 charges were laid. The incident had further repercussions for both concertgoers and bands alike as Ontario Place refused to book any punk or hard-rock bands for several years following Teenage Head's show.

But the riot proved a boom to Teenage Head, as sales of *Frantic City* surged by almost 10,000 in the three days following. In a 1992 CBC Radio interview, lead singer Frankie Venom said walking onto the Forum stage that night and hearing 15,000 young kids screaming and grabbing at the band's clothes was "better than any drug or alcohol I have ever done … I'll never forget it!"

BAD MANORS ON THE RADIO

Crowbar's *Bad Manors*, released in February 1971, features the Canadian classic "Oh What a Feeling," which was inducted into the Canadian Songwriters Hall of Fame in 2011 and holds the distinction of being the first-ever CanCon hit single. Not bad for a song that only features a couple of chords and some nonsensical lyrics ("Bop bada baa, Bop bada baa") to begin the tune. For those in the know, this made-up phrase had meaning; it was an inside joke and the password to gain entrance to Bad Manors — the six-bedroom farmhouse along Mohawk Road on Hamilton Mountain where Crowbar partied, wrote songs, rehearsed, and recorded this famous song and album.

Frank Davies, who produced *Bad Manors* and released it on his Daffodil Records label, shares another piece of little-known trivia about another song on the hit record.

> If you listen carefully during The Ghetto's blazing guitar solo on the *Bad Manors* track "Let the Four Winds Blow," you will hear lead singer Kelly Jay say, "Not that fucking guitar solo again," which has now been heard subliminally on radio thousands of times. Kelly was punching in his lead vocal over and over in the studio during the sessions for this particular song, and of course, we used the guitar solo as a cue for his entry/exit — to the point where on the 100th "take" he could take no more and emitted those immortal words. It sounded so natural. I just couldn't bear to take it out, so we buried it just under the track. The few of us who knew would smile every time we heard it!

TENT TINGLES

In the mid-1980s, after getting a tip about a French Canadian singer who was a megastar in her home province, Canadian producer David Foster flew to Montreal, then drove 150 kilometres in the rain to hear Céline Dion perform in a tent at an afternoon picnic in rural Quebec. Bad weather be damned. It played a part in this twist of fate that brought Foster and Dion together. Despite competing with the conversations of the audience, the singer's voice hit him immediately and Foster thought, "Millions and millions of people are going to love this woman." The music man was right. Foster ended up producing Dion's English-language debut, *Unison*, in 1990 and is credited with bringing her music to an audience outside the francophone world.

"Céline's the best singer I've ever worked with," Foster says of the five-time Grammy winner, with whom he notched another one of his 16 golden gramophones for *Falling into You* in 1996. "She was also incredible at taking direction. She knew her job, which was to sing. When it came to everything else, she just let others take care of it. Céline was the perfect artist. She had opinions, but she would try anything asked of her and that was golden."

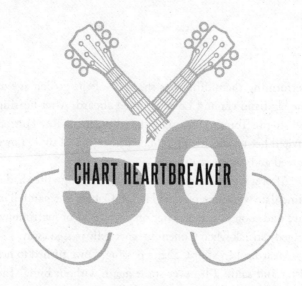

50 CHART HEARTBREAKER

Heartbreak led to a Canadian woman penning the first No. 1 song on Billboard's modern chart. "I'll Never Smile Again," written by 23-year-old Ruth Lowe in 1939, has been inducted into both the Canadian Songwriters Hall of Fame and the Grammy Hall of Fame. The song is a part of our country's deep well of treasured compositions.

Here's the story. At the tail end of the Great Depression — and as the world neared the outbreak of the Second World War — Lowe, in Toronto, wrote "I'll Never Smile Again." The sentimental ballad came to her following not just one, but two huge losses: the death of her father in 1932, followed by the passing of her husband in 1939.

Lowe had a natural gift for music. After her father died, she supported the family by selling her songs and by performing them. This was the start of the golden age of the big band era and Lowe climbed aboard. After hearing her sing in Toronto one night, bandleader Ina Ray Hutton invited her to join her all-female orchestra full time. Lowe agreed and hit the road.

After a gig one night in Chicago, the songwriter had a blind date with song plugger Harold Cohen. The pair fell in love and soon married. After only one year of matrimony, tragedy struck when Cohen unexpectedly passed away.

Heartbroken after Cohen's passing, Lowe turned to her sister and said, "I'll never smile again without him." The next day, she sat down at the piano and hastily wrote this haunting song.

Lowe shared the song with Toronto bandleader Percy Faith. He loved it. With the songwriter's permission, Faith arranged and recorded a 78 RPM single with his orchestra. Faith first broadcast the song in 1939 to CBC listeners on his regular program *Music by Faith*. But Lowe knew she had a hit on her hands beyond Canada. With the 78 in hand, the ambitious songwriter shared the recording and sheet music with bandleader Tommy Dorsey through his guitar player, who happened to be dating one of Lowe's friends at the time. Dorsey listened to "I'll Never Smile Again" and, like Faith, was moved.

He arranged a new version of the song with his band, and then brought it to Frank Sinatra and the Pied Pipers to record with him. The sentimental song ended up launching Sinatra's career; it was not only the crooner's first No.1 Billboard hit, but the first No. 1 record on Billboard's modern chart, staying atop it for 12 weeks, in 1941.

Like all great songs, "I'll Never Smile Again" stands the test of time and resonates with new generations. The composition inspired Frank Davies to create the Canadian Songwriters Hall of Fame. And, through the decades, "I'll Never Smile Again" has been covered by many artists, including Fats Waller, Sarah Vaughan, Billie Holiday, Big Joe Williams, Count Basie, Dave Brubeck, Oscar Peterson, Eddy Arnold, the Platters, Carl Perkins, Cleo Laine, Barry Manilow, and Michael Bublé. The song has also been frequently used in movies like *Good Morning, Vietnam* and *The Color of Money*. A pretty impressive legacy for a song written by a 23-year-old Toronto widow with a wounded heart.

51 RECORDING ON THE CHEAP

Here's a fun fact about Vancouver rock band 54-40 and their self-titled major-label debut, known as "the Green Album," and released in 1986. To save money, some of the demos were recorded on an old, discarded Bachman-Turner Overdrive outtake reel at Mushroom Studios in Vancouver (where Heart, Loverboy, and Sarah McLachlan also recorded albums). "We were sitting there saying, 'I hope this isn't a bit of history we are going over,' but it was $50 instead of $200 so damn right we were going to use it," says record co-producer Dave "Rave" Ogilvie.

The Green Album featured "I Go Blind" — a song that was a fan favourite and concert staple a decade before American soft rock band Hootie & the Blowfish covered it, releasing the song as the B-side to the Top 10 single "Hold

My Hand." In 1994, the cover became a radio hit, peaking at No. 2 on Billboard's Adult Top 40 chart and No. 22 on the Adult Contemporary chart. Later, it was added to the soundtrack to the popular sitcom *Friends*. While the writing of this song is a bit blurry for 54-40's lead singer Neil Osborne, he does recall jamming on it at bass player Brad Merritt's rehearsal space and taping it on a Pioneer 4-track reel-to-reel cassette. The song was inducted into the Canadian Songwriters Hall of Fame in 2021. The irony of the "I Go Blind" story is that Warner Brothers did not release it as a single, but radio knew a great song when they heard it and started playing it anyway — allowing it to hit No. 13 on Canada's RPM chart with very little promotion. The royalties from this song's success allowed 54-40 to build their own recording studio in Vancouver.

52 PARTNERSHIP IN SONG GOING STRONG

More than forty years on, McCartney and Lennon, Jagger and Richards, and John and Taupin are the most famed songwriting duos in rock. But Canada has also had its share of famous songwriting partners, starting in the 1960s with Randy Bachman and Burton Cummings, but few have lasted as long as the partnership of Bryan Adams and Jim Vallance, who met by chance in Vancouver in 1978 — launching what is likely one of the longest-running partnerships in song in Canadian history. The pair were inducted together into the Canadian Songwriters Hall of Fame in 2022 in a formal ceremony at Massey Hall.

In 1978, Adams and Vallance met at a Vancouver music store when the pair were introduced by a mutual friend. At the time, Adams, a high-school dropout who had convinced his mom to let him spend his college savings on a grand piano and formed the glam-rock band Sweeney Todd instead, was 18 years old and still living at home. Vallance was the former drummer and principal songwriter of the Vancouver-based rock band Prism, who had success in the late 1970s and early 1980s. The pair clicked on that first meeting and got together a week later and wrote their first song. The hits co-written by this pair of Vancouverites started with the title track from Adams's 1983 album, *Cuts Like a Knife*, which peaked at No. 15 on the Billboard Hot 100 and spent 14 weeks on the charts. A year later, the pair followed up on this success — and then some — with *Reckless*. Six of the ten songs on the record were Top 15 singles on the Billboard Hot 100. It was the first album by a Canadian artist to sell one million units in Canada (not to mention it went on to sell more than 12 million worldwide) and the third single from *Reckless* ("Heaven") became Adams's first number one single — spending two weeks at the top spot on the U.S. Billboard charts in June 1985.

53 FUNNY MONEY TO PAPER NICKELS

Canadian Tire money was introduced back in 1958 and resembles real banknotes. The customer loyalty program allows patrons to use this "funny money" toward in-store purchases. Not long after online fundraising platforms like Kickstarter, GoFundMe, and Patreon started, Canadian songwriter Corin Raymond found another way to finance his art when he used these beloved bills featuring the tam-wearing Sandy McTire to pay for his record *Paper Nickels*.

Starting in 2011, Raymond raised $6,200 in Canadian Tire money in a unique campaign that started with a song. The bulk of the album was recorded at Toronto's Tranzac Club, along with his band the Sundowners. Raymond accepted Canadian Tire money as the entrance fee to their shows and the campaign took on a life of its own from these humble beginnings. To put together the elaborate CD package that resembles a small coffee-table collectible — 20 songs on two CDs accompanied by a 144-page booklet — Raymond turned to his fans. They responded.

The inspiration initially came from one of the album's signature songs "Don't Spend It Honey" with the line "Don't spend it honey / Not the Canadian Tire money / We saved it so long." Raymond co-wrote this song with Winnipeg songwriter Rob Vaarmeyer. People loved the song and started to give Raymond Canadian Tire money at all his gigs — from house concerts to his weekly Cameron House Thursday night shows to people seeing him on the streets of Toronto and handing him a bundle. Money came in the mail from all over Canada. Bars helped his cause — like one of Raymond's locals on Queen Street West, the Done Right Inn, which already had accepted Canadian Tire money at par in the bar since 1999 and were happy to donate what they received to the songwriter. The story even found its way south of the border and led to an interview with the *Wall Street Journal.*

Canada embraced this made-in Canada story and what Raymond dubbed "Tire Fever" caught on. When the campaign concluded, the songwriter had collected 32,000 Canadian Tire bills weighing approximately 60 pounds. Toronto's Rogue Music Lab (owned by James Paul) accepted

Canadian Tire money at par — which is how it came to be that Raymond raised the money to fund his record. The songwriter ended up coming a little over $1,000 short of the bill from the studio ($7,333.75), but he was happy to pay the difference. Later, Raymond turned this story into a one-man theatrical show called *The Great Canadian Tire Money Caper* to share with audiences the whole story and the songs that led to the wild adventure he took on the road. Only in Canada!

SHAKESPEARE ... MY BUTT

Shakespeare My Butt is an odd title indeed for a debut record, but it's also part of the story that illustrates the raison d'être of Toronto band Lowest of the Low. Lead singer Ron Hawkins recalls the origin of the title of this 1991 album that perennially makes best-of lists of the top Canadian records of all-time.

> As best as I can remember, we were sitting around trying to come up with a title and I looked across the room at a framed poster John [Arnott] had on the wall and said, "Does that say Shakespeare's brain?" Someone replied, "No, it says Shakespeare's butt!" Someone else added, "Shakespeare ...

my butt," and it was a slam dunk from there. We thought it was sort of off-sounding, and we were very much in a place where we downplayed the idea that our lyrics were art. We thought of them more like journalism. The poster actually had said Shakespeare's Britain.

ROLLING WITH THE TIDES

In August 2015, to give some lucky listeners (some 1,000 strong) a sneak peak of songs from her forthcoming record *Utopia*, Serena Ryder gave a concert at low tide at Fundy National Park. Ryder and her band set up on Herring Cove Beach. At high tide, there is no sign of the beach. At low tide, a temporary idyllic spot to tan is revealed. From high tide to low tide and back to high tide again usually takes six hours, so every minute counted in staging this unique concert. The stage was built at low tide and sound check done. Then dismantled as tide rolled in before setting it up again for the real show.

The event was co-hosted by CBC Music and Parks Canada. Concertgoers received wireless headphones courtesy of Sennheiser to hear the concert, since the band did not use amplifiers to avoid disturbing the ecosystem. Audience members heard exactly what the musicians heard in their ears.

A helicopter was needed to fly in all of the equipment and staging for the concert and to make this unique show work the concert needed to be timed exactly to the flow of the world's highest tides. To attend the show on the ocean floor where it took place, the audience took a shuttle bus to the top of Herring Cove and then took a more than 151-step staircase to the ocean floor below. At 5 p.m. Serena started her performance. The show was later broadcast as a one-hour TV special "Quietest Concert Ever: On Fundy's Ocean Floor."

An encore was not in the cards. As soon as Ryder finished her last song (all timed to the tides) the crew got to work to remove all the equipment from the beach before the tide rolled back in again.

An interesting footnote to the story: Brian Kobayakawa, the bass player in Serena's band, left shortly after the gig to fly home. When he got off the plane, Brian saw that there were a bunch of texts from the tour manager saying to give him a call … and "make sure you're sitting down." Brian immediately expected the worst … maybe someone had died. Instead, he learned that when their gear was being lifted out in mesh fishing nets, his bass fell out and into the ocean! Thankfully, a Moncton roadie jumped from shore, swam out, and brought it back in. The bass was sent to a guitar maker in Moncton who looked it over and said it was fine — only to be destroyed anyway in a car accident a few months later!

THE NAME GAME

Back in the 1960s, Mel Shaw (who went on to become the first president of the Canadian Academy of Recording Arts and Sciences, or CARAS) was a one-man music business in Calgary. The trail-blazing pioneer of the Canadian music industry hosted dance hops in Alberta's largest city and helped promote local talent. The first band he hooked up with and achieved success with were the Rebounds. Never heard of this six-piece band? Not surprising, as that name did not last long. Here's the story of how Shaw convinced them to change their name.

Calgary, circa 1960, was a boring town when it came to live music. With no local scene and few places for bands to play beyond high-school dances, Shaw set his sights elsewhere. He concocted the idea of taking a group to

England and contacted an agent there about bringing over some Canadian talent. This guy agreed and said, just raise $10,000 and get over here and I'll do the rest.

Shaw had tried a fundraiser with a band before, but it fell through. After hearing the Rebounds rehearse one day, the promoter decided the scheme still had legs; he went to the local Chamber of Commerce to try and rustle up the required funds. A smooth talker and negotiator, Shaw convinced a local oilman to pony up the money by promising that the band would go to England and promote the Calgary Stampede. How would they do this? By playing the part of rock 'n' roll cowboys, of course — dressed in full Western wear, including white Smithbilt stetsons and cowboy boots. The benefactor liked the idea but upped the ante to seal the deal — the band needed to change their name.

Drummer Kim Berly recalls that moment when Shaw returned to the studio with the good news about securing the $10,000.

> Mel comes to our rehearsal and says, "he's going to give us the money!" I got so excited … we were going to England! Mel paused, and then continued. "There is just one thing though, we have to promote Calgary and he wants us to change the name of the band."

I got a cold chill, looked at Mel and said:
"Not the Stampeders!" He replied, "Yesss!"
all aglow. "You guys are going to be rock 'n'
roll cowboys." I wanted to be a hip cool guy
with long hair and a Beatles jacket, so this
was not great news!

Despite the promise, the $10,000 never arrived, so the trip to England was off, but the name change worked out okay. Not long after the band had honed their sound with the rebranded moniker locally, it was time to seek success in Toronto. Shaw bought a used nine-passenger 1957 Cadillac limousine from Imperial Oil and, along with his wife and two toddlers, crammed the Stampeders into this charming chariot and headed east.

After nearly five years following the white line and playing every bar imaginable in Ontario and Quebec, the Stampeders (now just a trio of Berly, Rich Dodson, and Ronnie King) hit it big in 1971 with its debut *Against the Grain*. The album featured the hit "Sweet City Woman," which won a Juno for Single of the Year and reached No. 8 on the U.S. Billboard Hot 100. *Against the Grain* went on to sell more than one million copies.

The Stampeders would return to their roots years later, though. After breaking up in the late 1970s, Berly and King were reunited with Dodson (whom they had not spoken with in 15 years) by surprise in 1992 on the *Dini Petty Show* as part of a "Where Are They Now" series. This eventually led to the trio mending their differences and reuniting. Their first gig? Where else but the Calgary Stampede.

57

ANOTHER GUINNESS, PLEASE

Did you know the Weeknd admired punk rockers like Iggy Pop and the Ramones, not hip-hop artists, before he made his first mixed tape? The Canadian artist also holds four Grammy Awards and four Guinness World Records.

Born Abel Makkonen Tesfaye in Toronto in 1990, Abel's parents had immigrated to Canada from Ethiopia, but his father abandoned him when he was just two years old. His grandmother — who lived through the Ethiopian "Red Terror" and military junta after Emperor Haile Selassie's death — helped raise him while his mother worked multiple jobs. As a teenager, Abel was enrolled in French immersion at Samuel Hearne Middle School in Scarborough and attended Ethiopian Orthodox church where he was introduced to music.

At age 17, Abel was kicked out of school and not long after formed his first hip-hop duo Bulleez N Nerdz; his rap name then was Kin Kane. His next group was XO, formed with his roommates, and that's when he adopted the moniker the Weeknd. Initially, he wanted to be called the Weekend, but there was already a rock band with that name. So, to avoid any legal trouble, he just dropped an *e*.

The Weeknd joined elite company following the release of "Can't Feel My Face" and "The Hills" from his 2015 record *Beauty Behind the Madness*, when he became only the 12th artist to score back-to-back number ones on the U.S. charts. This breakthrough for the Weeknd from his second studio album earned him a pair of Guinness World Records in the 2017 edition of the annual publication: the album was the most streamed on Spotify in one year (60 million unique listeners from December 1, 2014, to December 1, 2015) and the record that year for most consecutive weeks (45) in the Top 10 of Billboard's Hot 100 by a solo male artist.

The Weeknd added another pair of Guinness World Records in the 2020 and 2023 editions with a pair of hit singles for being the Biggest Selling Digital Single: "Blinding Lights" in 2020 was streamed almost 1.6 billion times and "Save Your Tears" had 2.15 billion "subscription streams equivalent" worldwide.

THAT NEW YEAR'S GUY

Long before it became a New Year's Eve trad-
ition sung across North America as the clock struck midnight, "Auld Lang Syne" was being played by Canada's
greatest dance-band leader Guy Lombardo and his Royal
Canadians to end their sets during their earliest gigs at
places like the Stork Club in Port Stanley, Ontario.

The Scottish folk song, now identified as the song sung
as people clink glasses, embrace, and wish each other Happy
New Year, was always sung by big bands to mark when
something ends, so it was the appropriate tune to close a
show with. Translated, it means "for old times' sake."

How did this tradition begin? Flash back to 1929.
Lombardo, who was born in London, Ontario, and his
group, the Royal Canadians, had become one of the hottest

big bands in North America. They got a winter residency in New York City playing the Roosevelt Hotel. That's where a wider audience started to hear "Auld Lang Syne." It was not just heard by the lucky few who got a table in the Roosevelt Grill, but it was broadcast first on radio and later on television from the fabled Manhattan hotel for the next 30 years.

Today "Auld Lang Syne" is still played on Dick Clark's New Year's Rockin' Eve celebrations and in houses, bars, and parties across North America. Lombardo passed away in 1977 and the Roosevelt closed for good in 2020 (a victim of the Covid-19 pandemic), but the legacy he left still lingers. Lombardo's *Time* obituary testifies to this fact: "His New Year's Eve concerts in New York City, which began in 1929, became an institution. First on radio, then TV, Lombardo's rendition of 'Auld Lange Syne' [*sic*] marked the nation's rite of passage from the old year to the new."

59

TORONTO LIGHTS UP FOR LENNON

Tickets were $6. The idea was a nod to the early pioneers of rock 'n' roll — bring back those 1950s stars who blazed a trail for the classic rock 'n' roll renaissance of the 1960s and 1970s. The date: September 13, 1969. The venue: Toronto's Varsity Stadium. On the bill, promoted as the Toronto Rock and Roll Revival, were the legends of rock: Chuck Berry, Little Richard, Gene Vincent, Jerry Lee Lewis, and Bo Diddley. These were the cats that influenced the likes of the Beatles and the Rolling Stones. The Doors and the Alice Cooper band were also on the bill.

One week to the show, only 2,000 tickets had been sold of the 10,000 required to break even. The concert, funded by the Eaton family, needed to come up with a Hail Mary to save the show. Twenty-five thousand ended up attending, most from Michigan, thanks to promotion there by a local DJ.

So how did a Toronto concert sell out to a crowd from Michigan? It started when 22-year-old promoter John Brower cold-called the office of John Lennon's Bag Productions to tell him of all the legendary acts booked and ask if he would consider being emcee. Lennon responded that he would not come unless he could play with Yoko and his new band that included guitarist Eric Clapton, future YES drummer Alan White, and artist Klaus Voormann on bass. Brower readily agreed to have Lennon play at the show instead.

Toronto's CHUM Radio did not believe Brower when he tried to use this news to sell tickets to salvage the concert. So, not getting the support locally, Brower passed the news on to fellow rock promoter Russ Gibb, who had a club in Detroit called the Grande Ballroom and hosted a radio show in Ann Arbor, Michigan. Gibb shared the news on air, which ended up selling 10,000 tickets in Detroit and Ann Arbor in just three days.

The performance was the first public one by Lennon and his new group the Plastic Ono Band following the breakup of the Fab Four earlier in the year. Upon arrival in Toronto, the band was escorted from Pearson Airport by a motorcade of 80 bikers from the Vagabonds.

Lennon was incredibly nervous, as he had not performed in several years during the Beatles' break, before their official breakup later that year. Emcee Kim Fowley, who was an L.A. record producer, saw Lennon's extreme stage fright and told the audience to "get out your matches and lighters, please. In a minute, I'm going to bring out John Lennon and Eric Clapton, and when I do, I want you to light them and give them a huge Toronto welcome." A new concert tradition was born.

THE MAKING OF AN '80S ANTHEM

The Parachute Club's "Rise Up," from the Toronto band's self-titled debut, was one of the first Canadian pop hits to include Caribbean rhythms of soca and reggae. In 1984, the song won the Juno for Single of the Year — beating out Bryan Adams ("Cuts Like a Knife" and "Straight from the Heart"), Corey Hart ("Sunglasses at Night"), and Men Without Hats ("The Safety Dance").

Lorraine Segato and drummer Billy Bryans had played in rock band Mama Quilla II in the late 1970s; this core eventually evolved into the Parachute Club in the 1980s. They had developed a following in Toronto's Queen Street West arts scene, which led to a demo deal. Seeking inspiration — and to broaden their musical horizons — Segato and Bryans spent one month in Trinidad with a friend of theirs to study and soak up soca music, a popular Trinidadian style that combines the soul of calypso with African and East Indian rhythms. Upon their return to Toronto, the Caribbean sounds seeped into the Parachute Club's music. Jamming in rehearsal one day, the melody and groove for "Rise Up" arrived in a moment of spontaneity. A true collaborative effort, Lauri Conger and Steve Webster added musical ideas to the melodies already penned by Bryans and Segato.

The words to match still eluded Segato until her best friend at the time — artist and poet Lynne Fernie, who was the unofficial eighth member of the band — made a suggestion based on the melody that echoed the theme of empowerment. Fernie felt the song needed the right words to match.

"Rise Up" was the last song they recorded in Daniel Lanois's Hamilton studio and Segato recalls how the final words to "Rise Up" just flowed out.

> I looked at Lynne's lyrics. I was in the studio with three pieces of paper … three different sets of lyrics and I was just cutting and pasting as I was singing. It was very spontaneous adding that final layer. We immediately realized what the song was about: empowerment and equality, but it also came from a deeply

spiritual place as well. Lynne had taken a drive up the B.C. coast and was touched by all of the indigenous ceremonial places you passed along the highway and something about the land spoke to her. The line "Rise Up and Share your power" part came from a feeling that was invoked on that trip.

Lanois added the final layers to the song, using his sonic genius, and created the dynamic intro. Segato still often thinks about this song and what a gift it was.

Timing is everything for a song and you can't ever plan that … you never know when you are going to hit a zeitgeist moment; we hit that moment where there was a confluence of all these energies: the energy of the street and the energy of the city [Toronto] and country rapidly and radically changing. There was also the influence created by the influx of immigrants from the Caribbean and elsewhere. That all affected the music of the street and that era.

Fittingly, with lyrics such as "We want freedom to love who we please" and "Want to love / Run wild in the streets," the song made its public debut at the 1983 Toronto Pride parade. Gay rights were still far from equal in society and under the law, and "Rise Up" was born out of the group's grassroots gay, lesbian, and feminist community.

TOILET ROCKERS TAKE ON FREE SPEECH

A sibling comedy duo, born and raised in the coal-
mining town of Glace Bay, Nova Scotia, known for their crude
songs like "I've Seen Pubic Hair" and "Dolly Parton's Tits,"
MacLean & MacLean released their debut, *Toilet Rock*, which
was produced by Lighthouse drummer Skip Prokop, in 1974.

Here's a story of staid Ontario and archaic laws.
Following the release of *Toilet Rock*, the duo was scheduled
to do a 100-date tour opening for Lighthouse. One night
in Swift Current, Saskatchewan, early in the tour, a local
reverend's son heard them drop the f-bomb onstage. All
hell broke loose. The media picked up the story. Suddenly,
MacLean & MacLean were national news.

The next thing you know, cops showed up at the duo's
shows with tape recorders to catch them in the act of using

that four-letter word on stage. Ludicrous you say? Definitely in an age where you can walk by a school playground and hear a kindergarten kid shout the F-word. But back in the 1970s, after some inspectors from the Ontario Liquor Board caught their profanity-filled show in London, Ontario, they enforced laws that prohibited pub owners from hiring the duo. The pair challenged this edict on the grounds it was not only an infringement on their right to freedom of speech, but it also prevented them from working and earning a living.

Civil rights activist and constitutional lawyer Clayton Ruby took on MacLean & MacLean's case. Despite the distraction caused by police surveillance at their shows, the pair kept on working — and repeatedly breaking this ridiculous law — just to pay Ruby's legal fees! An early guilty verdict in Ontario provincial court was appealed and went all the way to the Supreme Court. Finally, the comedians won — a victory for freedom of speech. They could smile as they gave the proverbial middle finger back to those staid bureaucrats who tried to ban their art.

FARMING LIFE LESSONS

Released in 1991, Loreena McKennitt's *The Visit* is one of those "happy accidents." The record won the Stratford, Ontario, artist a Juno the following year for Best Roots and Traditional Album of the Year and took the artist and her band around the globe. At a time when techno, hip hop, and alternative rock dominated the airwaves, somehow McKennitt's collection of Celtic-influenced songs played on her harp, inspired by Shakespeare, Japanese cultural traditions, and Romantic poets, and marked by the use of interesting instruments like the balalaika and tamboura, found an audience, selling 1.4 million copies worldwide.

The album was distributed by Warner Music Canada in a deal that was unlike anything a major label had agreed to before with an artist. Referred to in the industry as the

"Loreena McKennitt deal," it was basically more of a partnership. McKennitt financed the album recorded at Jeff Wolpert's Inception Studios in Toronto. It was then licensed to the Warner Music Canada label, which used its resources and expertise to handle distribution of the record once it was ready — helping the singer-songwriter reach untapped international markets. This meant that McKennitt, who took pride in her independence, kept responsibility for financing her records and her tours, and Warner Music Canada invested little and took on very little risk in the transaction. By the time McKennitt was set to record *The Visit*, she had realized that she needed help with distribution, as record stores could not keep her music in stock, and she could not manufacture enough to meet the demand.

Where did McKennitt learn how to run a business? From lessons in skills such as accounting and marketing from her livestock dealer father while growing up in Winnipeg, Manitoba.

WHEN TEARS WERE NOT ENOUGH

In the mid-1980s, Ethiopia was in the middle of a two-year drought. The resulting prolonged famine caused nearly one million deaths. The world wept seeing photos of emaciated children in this African nation. As an all-star group of Canadian musicians sang, tears wouldn't be enough to help these people.

The Brits were the first to lend a hand. The U.K.-based supergroup Band Aid, organized by Boomtown Rats lead singer Bob Geldof, brought light to this plight with their song: "Do They Know It's Christmas?" Released in December 1984, the song became the fastest selling single of all-time in the U.K.

Inspired by Geldof's fundraiser, Harry Belafonte spearheaded a U.S. supergroup called U.S.A. for Africa.

The band's charity song, "We Are the World," written by Michael Jackson and Lionel Richie, sold more than 20 million copies. Quincy Jones, who produced the American hit, contacted David Foster and urged Canada to rally behind the Ethiopian famine cause and record a Canadian version to raise more money.

So, in 1985, on a cold Sunday in February, Canadian music history was made at Manta Sound studios in downtown Toronto. For one afternoon, with Ethiopians on their minds, a who's who of musical talent, more than 50 strong, checked their egos at the door and sang their hearts out, screaming to the world. Actors like John Candy, Catherine O'Hara, and Eugene Levy, and National Hockey League stars like Wayne Gretzky also added their voices and time to the cause as part of the choir.

Organizers of the "Tears Are Not Enough" session tried to keep the location a secret from the press (and public), but even in an age long before social media, people found out — and turned out. Screaming teenagers, hoping for a Corey Hart or Bryan Adams sighting, lined the sidewalk on Adelaide Street and crowded close to the entrance outside Manta Sound. Once inside, Foster led the supergroup, dubbed the Northern Lights, which included legends like Anne Murray, Joni Mitchell, Oscar Peterson, Neil Young, and Gordon Lightfoot. Foster composed the music, with Jim Vallance and Bryan Adams adding the lyrics. Released as a single in March 1985, it reached No. 1 on the Canadian charts and sold more than 300,000 copies — raising more than $3.2 million for famine relief.

A fun fact about these sessions: Foster told both Neil Young and Joni Mitchell (who had arrived together in a taxi) that they were out of tune. Young replied to the producer's assessment in typical Neil style: "That's my sound man!" Foster still made the future Rock and Roll Hall of Famer do 13 takes and Mitchell do 10 takes.

64

ODE TO AN AIRPORT

A four-minute and 25-second instrumental on Rush's eighth studio album, *Moving Pictures*, "YYZ" is one of the most challenging songs the Canadian power-trio played, but it was always also one of the most enjoyable to play and a staple of their live shows. Co-written by Geddy Lee and Neil Peart, the song was nominated for a Grammy Award in the Best Rock Instrumental category in 1982. Lee once described the birth of this song as a "bass and drum extravaganza" since guitarist Alex Lifeson was not in the room and Lee and Peart just started to jam.

Why "YYZ"? The song is an ode to their hometown of Toronto — YYZ is the International Air Transport Association code for the city's Pearson International Airport. The composition gathers all the emotions of what the airport meant to the band and to their careers — homecomings, goings, and a place rich in symbolism of the exotic and the nostalgic. These feelings all appear in the many moods of this musical masterpiece. According to Lifeson, the idea for the iconic opening riff came when he was flying the band home in a small aircraft back to Toronto from Le Studio in Montreal for a break in the *Moving Pictures* sessions. As they approached Toronto, a flight instructor friend who had tagged along with the band tuned the inflight radio into the local identifier. The rhythm of this Morse code of dots and dashes resonated and felt really melodic to the band. "YYZ" was born. The opening of the song is played in a 10/8 time signature and the Y-Y-Z in Morse code is repeated several times using various musical arrangements. Lee explained the meaning of this song in a DVD that accompanied the deluxe version of *Moving Pictures* to celebrate the album's 40th anniversary: "We'd see that YYZ on our ticketed bags and it was always really exciting. We're coming home. We wanted to put together a song about that. Even though it's instrumental, it's about our town, kinda where we came from."

CANADIAN "GAL" TAKES OVER

In 1996, singer-songwriter Sarah McLachlan was fed up. Sexism in the music industry was rampant, and she had heard the word "no" one too many times. The males-in-charge at radio stations at the time were telling McLachlan when she went into their studios that they could not add her new song to their playlists or put it into rotation since they already had a song by another female artist, and they refused to play two songs by women in a row.

"I'll show you!" McLachlan shouted back at the industry, which she did by founding Lilith Fair, an all-female music festival named by one of McLachlan's closest friends after a mythological deity that represents independence from men and a desire for female autonomy.

Even before the festival was announced, McLachlan faced opposition from male music-industry executives and concert bookers and promoters who told her there was no way a lineup that featured more than one woman on the bill would succeed. Music-industry insiders mocked the festival, calling it "Lesbopalooza."

The festival opened on July 5, 1997, at the Gorge Amphitheatre in George, Washington state, and sold out — 15,000 strong. Sellouts happened in the other cities, too: 30,000 attended in some stops, including the Greek Theatre in Los Angeles; the Shoreline Amphitheatre in Mountain View, California; and Thunderbird Stadium in Vancouver. In that first year, Lilith Fair had 37 shows across North America that featured 69 women-fronted acts. The lineup of the founding festival, besides McLachlan, included Sheryl Crow, Jewel, Indigo Girls, Lisa Loeb, Fiona Apple, Shawn Colvin, Tracy Chapman, Natalie Merchant, and many more. Ticket sales that first summer outsold the Lollapalooza festival. And McLachlan, hugging her guitar, made the cover of *Time* with the caption "The Gals Take Over."

The gauntlet had been thrown. Lilith Fair ran for two more years and featured nearly 300 women artists. Over its three-year run, more than 1.5 million attended these shows and Lilith Fair ended up the top-grossing music festival of the late '90s — selling more than $60 million in ticket sales alone over three years.

Not only a financial success, the festival also introduced audiences to new acts and helped the careers of many artists including fellow Canadians Nelly Furtado and Tegan and Sara. Jewel and Dido both saw their careers skyrocket following their appearances at Lilith Fair. The festival was also a connector for many female artists from different genres and eras — providing the opportunity for acts like Queen Latifah and Bonnie Raitt to meet for the first time.

MADD FOR SODA

In 1984, Canadian rock musician Kim Mitchell released "Go for Soda" from his first solo record, *Akimbo Alogo*. The three-minute and 25-second song from the former lead singer of Max Webster became a party anthem. The song was Mitchell's only single that charted in the U.S. on the Billboard Hot 100, reaching No. 86 and climbing no higher when it was overtaken by Twisted Sister's "We're Not Gonna Take it."

The song also found its way into American pop culture in several ways: *Miami Vice* — one of the hottest TV shows at the time — used the song to lead off one of their episodes; and the Coca-Cola Company borrowed the song to promote its cherry-flavoured soft drink, Mr. Pibb.

But the most famous endorsement came from Mothers Against Drunk Driving (MADD) south of the border who adopted "Go for Soda" for one of their anti-drinking-and-driving campaigns.

Mitchell later said the song had nothing to do with teetotalling. Not really surprising when you consider the songwriter also penned the drinking songs "Lager and Ale" and "I Am a Wild Party." Mitchell tweeted this in a reply to a fan asking about the song's meaning: "Go For Soda was never about drinking ... it's a song about two ppl [*sic*] in conflict ... they can't resolve anything so they 'might as well go for soda' ... nobody hurts cries drowns or dies.... hint >> listen to the verses ;)"

A PROMOTER'S PAYDAY

Managing egos. Negotiating contracts with artists, managers, and venues. The devil is in the details. That's a concert promoter's job in a nutshell. The ones who put on the show are also the ones who take on the most financial risk. Landing on the right budget is key and involves so many factors that there is always a little luck involved in finalizing this complex formula of determining the right price to pay the artist, the right price to charge, and marketing the event to the right audience at the right time. In his memoir *True North: A Life in the Music Business*, Canadian music executive Bernie Finkelstein explains how "the concert business" works:

> Using rough figures, let's say the theatre has
> 2,000 sellable seats at $50 a head. That's

$100,000 coming in for a full house. There are all kinds of deals out there but, to make it simple, let's say the performer's take from the show amounts to 60 per cent. That's $60,000. The other $40,000 goes toward the costs, including the hall rental, advertising, staff and crew charges, catering, the promoter's profit, and ... well, the list can be endless. A manager might be taking somewhere between 15 and 25 per cent of that $60,000 ... In the end, if you're in the music business for the money, you're in the wrong business. Still, it could pay, and when it did, it paid out quite nicely, thank you very much.

Elliott Lefko, president of concert promotion company Goldenvoice, always knew he would end up in the music business. During his formative years, he clipped out ads of upcoming shows, and while in high school started promoting shows. After seeing Canadian troubadour Ray Materick open for José Feliciano at Massey Hall, he was so blown away that he called up the Riverboat, where Materick was a regular, to get the songwriter's number from owner Bernie Fiedler. Lefko's first show was bringing Materick to his high school. A career was launched. Since then, he's promoted thousands of shows, including the first Toronto appearances by Nirvana.

Lefko shares an anecdote about how even when you believe you've got the right act, the right price, and the right venue, there is still no rhyme or reason sometimes to the promotion game.

After learning about Stax Records' legendary father-daughter duo Rufus and Carla Thomas from his York University professor Rob Bowman, Lefko booked them at the Horseshoe Tavern.

The pair were legends in the 1960s, but by the mid-1980s when Lefko booked them, no one apparently remembered. The Shoe was empty that night and Lefko had been relying on ticket sales to pay the band. Lefko did not have enough money, so went downstairs to Kenny Sprackman's office (one of the Horseshoe owners at the time) and told Kenny his story. Sprackman knew the tale well, as he had previously booked shows at the Isabella Hotel. He took out his chequebook and told the promoter to go up to the bar and let them know how much he needed, and they would cash it for him.

Just a week later Lefko was back at the Horseshoe promoting an unknown zydeco band. The show sold out. Now flush with cash, the promoter repaid Sprackman. The lesson Lefko learned was this: "That is the business I'm in. It's all risk! Promoters usually do what they do because they love music and love the acts, but unfortunately that is not always the best recipe for success."

THE CRACK OF DAWN

White supremacists in Toronto in the mid-1970s often made it difficult for Black artists to play in clubs as they stirred up their supporters — especially racist neo-Nazi sympathizer groups like the Western Guard.

Crack of Dawn, an R&B, funk disco, and soul group founded in Toronto in 1975 and still playing today after several hiatuses, was one of the groups that faced this blatant display of racism and were attacked by their audience. Although the band featured a bunch of new immigrants from Jamaica and the West Indies, who brought with them their island influences and mixed it with a burgeoning and distinct Toronto R&B sound and rehearsed in Toronto's Little Jamaica neighbourhood, they played gigs at establishments where people of colour at that time were often not welcome or allowed, such as country clubs and certain saloons. Band member Trevor Daley was even shot in the head in 1975 as he entered the Generator — a disco tavern at Yonge and Eglinton. Learn more about these trailblazers in the documentary *Paving the Way: The Crack of Dawn Story*.

69

TV THEME KING

When Canadians think about the late great Alan Thicke, musical composer is not the first thing that comes to mind. Born in Kirkland Lake, Ontario, Thicke was better known as an actor and producer — especially for his long-running role on the hit TV comedy *Growing Pains*.

What many might not know is that the actor began his career as a writer for CBC Television and went on to compose more than 40 TV theme songs, including those for some of the most popular sitcoms from the late 1970s and early 1980s such as *Diff'rent Strokes* and *The Facts of Life*. For these compositions, which Thicke co-wrote with his first wife, Gloria Loring, and TV producer Al Burton, he was inducted into the Canadian Songwriters Hall of Fame in 2020.

A SIGN OF THE TIMES

Sam Sniderman started selling records in 1937 at his store Sniderman Radio Sales & Service in a stand-alone department called Sniderman's Music Hall at 714 College Street in Toronto. Vinyl was stacked and crammed in the small, rundown space. By the late 1950s Sam's had one of the largest collections of recordings in the world and had changed the name of the store to Sam the Record Man, more commonly known as Sam's.

A&A Records, another family-run record store, was Sam's chief competitor and the Snidermans moved to Yonge Street, relocating in the basement of Yolles Furniture, to better compete with A&A. In 1961, Sam relocated his business again, to 347 Yonge Street — just a few footsteps away from A&A. In those days, this stretch of Yonge Street was a movie district and Sam's stayed open until midnight to catch the moviegoers before they headed home. The tactic worked. In 1967, Sam's annual sales topped $2 million.

In 1969, Sam decided the store needed more exposure. The businessman hired sign makers the Brothers Markle to create a large vinyl sign that resembled two spinning records. In the decades to come, this flashing spinning neon sign that was 15 metres by 10 metres was a beacon on the Yonge Street strip. Sales surged.

Sniderman franchised his store and at its height there were 130 Sam the Record Man stores across Canada. The walls of the Yonge location were covered with Gold Records by Canadian artists. By 2002, through expansion, the retailer was 40,000 square feet and carried 400,000 titles.

Sam's clientele also included Canadian musicians, many of whom became his friends over the years and performed at the flagship location. It was not unusual for the likes of Stompin' Tom Connors, Gordon Lightfoot, or Anne Murray to stop by and play a few songs.

Sam's, along with A&A, were both victims of the changing music industry and the way people consumed music as streaming killed the LP industry in the late 1990s and early 2000s. Ryerson University (now Toronto Metropolitan University) purchased both buildings, which were demolished to create a new facility for students.

Today, after spending more than a decade in storage, and thanks to being named a protected heritage element by the City of Toronto, the iconic Sam the Record Man sign is all that remains — it has been installed permanently on a building that overlooks Yonge–Dundas Square. In 2012, Canada lost a music industry giant when Sam Sniderman passed away at the age of 94.

71
WHAT NOT TO DO AT SXSW

This story, shared by Lowest of the Low singer Ron Hawkins, is a warning to young artists of what not to do when you are invited to Austin, Texas, to play South by Southwest (SXSW).

In the early 1990s, Lowest of the Low was riding high after the indie success of their debut, *Shakespeare My Butt*, and were scheduled to play at the biggest music festival in North America. Instead of "keeping their eye on the prize," as Hawkins says, the Canadian musicians played the stereotypical part of spoiled, selfish rock stars by spending their Texas days and nights partying — taking illicit drugs and drinking to excess.

After somehow getting through customs, the band arrived in downtown Austin. Walking along Sixth Street,

Hawkins opened his wallet to discover a piece of tinfoil with six hits of acid wrapped inside. This was a harbinger. He and his bandmates consumed the evidence rather than risk taking it back to Canada. The debauchery began.

Lowest of the Low stayed with a pair of college girls (apparently a SXSW tradition to billet artists in the early years so they did not have to pay for accommodations). Of course, these co-eds liked to party. The band performed two shows in three days but spent most of their time drunk and passed out on their billet's floor.

On the final day, Hawkins recalls cooking some blackened fish and washing it down with tequila and beer. Suddenly, he remembered they had a plane to catch. The band and their crew frantically packed and arrived at the airport, still inebriated, with little time to spare.

While waiting for their plane to take off, they kept the party going. Another lesson learned. Their sound technician sat in a balsam-framed window in one of the restaurants and fell through — causing a commotion and prompting the arrival of police and airport security. The band's manager talked to the cops, who were ready to arrest the crazy Canucks on the spot for public drunkenness and disorderly conduct. Somehow, the manager convinced the Texas authorities to let the musicians board the plane. He reasoned that then they would be Canada's problem!

Cop cars were even on the runway to make sure the plane left without further incident. To this day, Lowest of the Low are banned from playing anywhere in the Lone Star State.

72 MUCH COMES OUT

In June 1999, Denise Donlon was vice-president and general manager at the nation's music station, MuchMusic. The philanthropist and music industry trailblazer, who went on to become president of Sony Music Canada from 2000 to 2004, still smiles when she recalls the significance of what she and her Much colleagues did that June by standing up, supporting, and championing human rights. The act: becoming the first mainstream broadcaster to put a float in Toronto's Pride Day parade.

"We were a private broadcaster, yet in many ways, we acted more like a public one," Donlon recalls. "Part of my reason to get up in [the] morning back then was not to play Metallica videos, but to use the station as an environment that was welcoming to all and reflected cultural diversity."

Much Comes Out became the tag line/slogan that announced the broadcaster's decision to participate and enter a float in the annual parade. The idea came from MuchMusic employee Gregory Hewitt, who one day said to Donlon: "The Toronto Pride Day Parade is coming up. Wouldn't it be amazing if Much had a float?" The wheels started to turn. Donlon got buy-in from the other executives, the owners of the station, and the majority of staff. Some of the on-air personalities volunteered to be on the float, which would also include *Electric Circus* dancers.

Immediately after announcing the "Much Comes Out" initiative, Donlon, along with the station, received dozens of calls filled with homophobic slurs and threats. The broadcast executive was rattled and afraid — not wanting to put anyone in danger — but president of CHUM Television Ron Waters was 100 percent behind the initiative, telling Donlon, "We've got your back!"

The float went ahead as planned. Extra security was hired and the day of the parade the float was ready. Donlon laughs today recalling what they had created. The *Electric Circus* dancers all wore glitter and boas, and the float was outfitted with yards of Astroturf with a centrepiece: two massive papier-mâché legs mounted and spread-eagle on either side of a large MuchMusic logo. The float queen was Tim Taylor, an assistant who worked in the creative services department. Donlon still remembers trying to find a sewing kit to secure in place the two tennis balls inside Taylor's halter top just before he got on the float.

Though it rained that morning, the sun shone by the time the parade started. "We danced down Yonge Street all giddy and excited to celebrate the whole rainbow," says Donlon. "I remember seeing kids in strollers watching the parade and thinking now they are probably in their 20s ... I hope we influenced them and the MuchMusic audience because love won that day; it triumphed over hate and that day changed the way I spoke about inclusivity for the rest of my career."

A "SUGAR-COATED FELLATIO FEST"

Everyone knows the names of famous best-selling boy bands from the United States like New Kids on the Block, Boyz II Men, NSYNC, and Backstreet Boys. Did you know Canada also produced a few of these teenage heartthrob groups? Here's one.

B4-4 (later known as Before Four) was a Toronto trio that featured twins Ryan and Dan Kowarsky and Ohad Einbinder. Formed in 1998, Sony's Mike Roth heard B4-4 audition in Sony's lobby. The A&R representative was en route to a meeting and the boys were harassing the receptionist that they needed to "sing for someone." Roth bailed her out and agreed to hear the trio sing — telling them he was the delivery person. The song and the rest is history.

The boy band achieved commercial success in Canada thanks to the single "Get Down" — which became infamous for its suggestive lyrics that reference oral sex. MuchMusic's crude puppet Ed the Sock mocked the song in his annual *Fromage* roundup in 2000 highlighting the cheesiest videos of the year, calling the song a "sugar-coated fellatio fest!"

But the kids didn't seem to be bothered by the meaning behind the lyrics. Canadian songwriter Jessie Reyez revealed on social media that due to the lewd lyrics, of which she was unaware, her high-school principal prevented her from covering a B4-4 song in the talent show.

TAKE OFF, EH!

Bob and Doug McKenzie made their TV debut on September 19, 1980. The pair of fictional "hoseheads" was created by Canadian actors Dave Thomas and Rick Moranis for the sketch comedy series *SCTV*. The *SCTV* segment that took into account all of the Canadian stereotypes was originally called "Kanadian Korner," and later changed to "Great White North."

The inspiration for the segment came when U.S. producers, who needed to add two extra minutes to the show to fit it into the time slot on CBC, asked Moranis and Thomas to create a spot with "Canadian content." The comedy duo thought this was a joke as the entire *SCTV* show was filled with Canadian content! It was set in Canada, filmed in Canada, and had an all-Canadian cast.

What did they do? What any comedians would, they decided to have some fun and give their audiences "cultural content" from north of the 49th parallel in the form of stereotypes: beer, doughnuts, and back bacon ... and a language marked by insults like "hoser" and the liberal use of "eh," which apparently all Canadians say in phrases like "Take off, eh."

The duo filmed the segment at the end of one day of shooting for the rest of the series. They drank real beer and most of the dialogue was ad libbed. Sporting toques, scarves, plaid shirts, and bulky parkas — Bob and Doug satirized all things Canadian while drinking stubby beers.

In 1981, Anthem Records (label home to Rush) signed the pair and released their debut record, *Great White North*. The lead single "Take Off" featured Rush front man and bassist Geddy Lee providing guest vocals. The album sold more than one million copies and reached No. 16 on the Billboard Hot 100 and was even nominated for a Grammy Award. The record also featured a reworking of the classic Christmas carol "The Twelve Days of Christmas" — replacing the normal gifts with Canadiana like French toast instead of French hens and turtlenecks instead of turtle-doves. And of course, on the first day of Christmas they got a beer.

The duo kept the momentum going by putting together a full-length feature film — *Strange Brew* — in 1983.

While the movie was more of a cult classic and a modest hit, making approximately $4 million at the box office, the movie's soundtrack won a Juno Award for Comedy Album of the Year.

THE GREATEST JAZZ CONCERT *EVER*

May 15, 1953, is a date that many critics today consider the day the "the greatest jazz concert ever" happened. At the time, it was just another Friday night at Toronto's Massey Hall.

The all-star quintet is what made this concert the greatest ever held in this genre. It was the only time that five of the universally acknowledged top jazz cats of the bebop tradition — alto saxophonist Charlie Parker, trumpeter Dizzy Gillespie, pianist Bud Powell, bassist Charles Mingus, and drummer Max Roach — shared the stage. These legends offered a loose and spontaneous 47-minute set that consisted of only six tunes and part of a seventh.

But 600 of a possible 2,700 seats in the theatre were sold. The night of the show, most of North America was glued to their TV sets and radios to take in the heavy-weight boxing match between Rocky Marciano and Jersey Joe Walcott. Some feel this is one of the reasons tickets did not sell. In the *Globe and Mail* the next day, Alex Barris was lukewarm in his review of the show, describing it as a "two-and-a-half-hour clambake."

This Canadian concert became more famous in the following decades after a live recording of the show was released, first on three 10-inch LPs in 1956 called *Jazz at Massey Hall: The Quintet.* A promoter probably dreamt up the moniker in the early 1970s when Prestige Records re-released the recording and added the title *The Greatest Jazz Concert Ever.*

"SAFETY" DANCE IF YOU WANT TO

If you came of age in the MuchMusic era of the mid-1980s, you surely remember the video for Men Without Hats' huge hit "The Safety Dance." Directed by Tim Pope, who had made videos for British new wave bands like the Cure and the Psychedelic Furs, it featured British folk revival imagery and was filmed in the small English countryside village of West Kington. But what was a "safety dance" and how did Ivan Doroschuk, the lead singer of the Montreal band, come up with the song's famed tag line: "We can dance if we want to" for this 1982 protest anthem that cracked Top 10 charts in the U.S., the U.K., New Zealand, and South Africa?

Doroschuk wrote the protest song after getting kicked out one too many times from Montreal clubs in the dying days of disco for a dance deemed too dangerous. DJs, during the course of the night, would slip in some Devo, a B-52's song like "Rock Lobster," or Blondie's "Heart of Glass." As soon as those songs began, Doroschuk and his friends would hit the floor and start to pogo dance. (Pogoing was the precursor to the mosh pit.) Nobody had seen that before. The bouncers thought they were fighting.

Reflecting on the mammoth hit years later, the Men Without Hats front man feels like the song is now way bigger than him or the band. "I feel like a museum curator travelling around the globe and presenting this musical artefact to people that procures immense joy."

BIG ACTS, LOW ATTENDANCE

Toronto is infamous for hosting historic concerts — including several mentioned in this book for records of attendance, or as the first place a new ritual began. But Canada's largest city has also hosted some shows memorable for another reason — artists' first shows, before they were known, to only a handful of people. Here's a trio:

1. Led Zeppelin at The Rockpile, February 2, 1969. Promoter John Brower, a young impresario who was also behind the Toronto Pop Festival and the Rock and Roll Revival later that same year, made Zeppelin's Toronto debut happen. The British band's self-titled debut had been released just a few weeks before in the U.S. The initial reviews of the record were

not that glowing. Maybe this played into the low attendance. According to Brower, who also co-owned the Rockpile (a club that was located inside the Masonic Temple building at Yonge and Davenport in the late 1960s), there were more people working at his club the night Zeppelin came to town than paying concertgoers. A few months later, following Woodstock, Led Zeppelin returned and played two sold-out shows.

2. The Police at the Horseshoe Tavern, November 2–3, 1978. Another gig where there were more staff in attendance than paying patrons. The Police were brought to town by the concert promotion duo of Gary Topp and Gary Cormier, better known to those in the music industry as "the Garys," to play two nights at the Shoe. The band felt so bad about the attendance that they gave the Garys back the $200 fee agreed to in their contract. This was another case of a band on the cusp of stardom. The promoters knew the band would be big, but the media and the public had not caught on yet to the uniqueness of this British trio's sound. Six months later, "Roxanne" was all over the radio waves.

3. Nirvana at Lee's Palace, April 16, 1990. The show was presented by Elliott Lefko and was part of the band's tour promoting their debut, *Bleach*. The grunge rockers from Seattle, led by Kurt Cobain, had yet to sign with a major label and the unexpected mainstream commercial success of "Smells Like Teen Spirit" — the first single from their second album, *Nevermind*, was still more than a year in the future. Dave Grohl had yet to replace original drummer Chad Channing. The band was paid $1,000 and only about 100 people showed up. Lore from this show is that Cobain put a table on stage and sat on it, then proceeded to launch beer bottles into the air near the close of their set, and the crowd reciprocated.

78
SQUARE-DANCE SINGER

Gordon Lightfoot is known for storied songs like "Early Morning Rain" — but did you know that the legendary Canadian songwriter got his start on television … clog dancing? Back in the early 1960s, Lightfoot was still finding his feet in the music business and taking whatever gigs he could to raise his profile. Television, being the best medium to reach the most people, felt like the right tool. The songwriter landed a spot as a country dancer on the CBC variety show *Country Hoedown*. And this was not just a one-off appearance. Lightfoot was a regular on the weekly TV show, clog dancing for more than two years, from 1960 to 1962, and harmonizing as a member of the Singin' Swingin' Eight.

In 1973, reflecting on this gig, Lightfoot told Elwood Glover why he landed a role on the TV show: "The only reason I was on *Country Hoedown* was because I was a crackerjack sight-reader, and I sang in the vocals chorus. As a matter of fact, I was probably the best singer and harmonizer on it, but every night they'd make us get out there and clog for a minute. That was part of the trip."

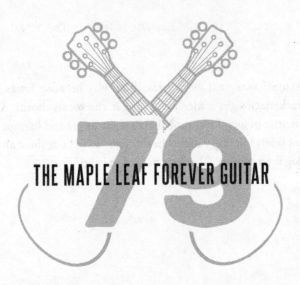

THE MAPLE LEAF FOREVER GUITAR

May 2014. Canadian musician Colin Cripps (Blue Rodeo, Crash Vegas, Junkhouse) and the MP from his Toronto riding met at a governor general's luncheon in Ottawa where Blue Rodeo were being honoured with a lifetime achievement award. Their conversation led to the creation of what became known as the Maple Leaf Forever Guitar.

A little background: in Toronto's east end stood a 170-year-old silver maple tree that inspired poet and song-writer Alexander Muir to write "The Maple Leaf Forever," in 1867 — unofficially considered Canada's first national anthem. In July 2013, a massive windstorm felled much of the tree. The fallen lumber was cut into pieces, placed in a kiln, and dried for nearly a year before it was tendered by the City of Toronto to projects that reflected the tree's place in our cultural history. Cripps, a vintage guitar collector, took the idea of building an acoustic guitar with the maple to his friend Dave Fox — a luthier based in Peterborough, Ontario.

The pair worked collaboratively to craft a beautiful instrument, which was finished in 2015. Today, it is passed on annually to a different musician — adding to the legacy from which the instrument was born and forever making sure it remains in the public trust.

This gorgeous guitar features a warm tone and sounds very "mahogany like," because silver maple wood is less dense than other varieties. The instrument weighs five pounds, six ounces, and the body features a Sitka spruce top with spalted maple rosette and a celluloid "tiger-stripe" vintage-style pickguard. The guitar's back and sides are made of silver maple from the Maple Leaf Forever Tree.

Other unique finishing details include twin maple leafs inlaid at the fifth fret, a 2014 "Maple Leaf Forever" $10 silver coin on the back of the headstock, and a vintage Canada luggage decal on the back of the body. Later, Cripps ended up working with luthier Tom Bartlett to build an electric guitar as well using wood from the Maple Leaf Forever Tree.

LET'S GO TO THE HOP ...

In the early 1960s, *American Bandstand* (which started in 1956 and ran until 1989) was one of the most popular TV shows for teenagers south of the border. Hosted by Dick Clark, the show featured live music and interviews with the latest rock 'n' roll stars in the making — giving acts like Ike & Tina Turner, the Beach Boys, Jerry Lee Lewis, and Stevie Wonder their first exposure to North American audiences. Canada decided to emulate this after-school music program with *Music Hop*, which aired its first episode on October 3, 1963.

The program ran on CBC Television from 1963 to 1967; it's where many future Canadian stars like Gordon Lightfoot were introduced to a wider audience and fuelled their success. Hosted by Alex Trebek for the first year and Dave Mickie (a pseudonym for AM radio DJ David Marsden) thereafter, the show featured house band Norm Amadio and the Rhythm Rockers, which included future Gordon Lightfoot band members guitarist Red Shea and bassist John Stockfish, and a live audience of teenyboppers who danced to the music. Starting in the second season, regional versions of *Music Hop* were created so there was a music show airing every weekday from one of Canada's major cities: on Mondays *Let's Go* from Vancouver, on Tuesdays *Jeunesse Oblige* from Montreal, on Wednesdays *Hootenanny* from Winnipeg, on Thursdays was the Toronto original version of *Music Hop*, and Fridays saw *Frank's Bandstand* coming from Halifax.

HEARTTHROB HART

"Sunglasses at Night," the first single from Corey Hart's debut, *First Offense*, is a song that changed his life. The video helped the teenage heartthrob reach international acclaim. The song peaked at No. 7 on the U.S. Billboard Hot 100 chart in September 1984.

The video was directed by Rob Quartly, who was the go-to guy for some of the earliest and most successful Canadian music videos for bands like the Spoons, Helix, and Platinum Blonde. Filmed at Toronto's Don Jail, the video begins with Hart sporting what became his famed Wayfarer Ray-Bans, getting arrested, and leaving with an officer played by future MuchMusic VJ Laurie Brown. The song won the Juno in the newly created Video of the Year category in 1984 and made Hart a household name.

RONNIE'S ROCK 'N' ROLL CAR

Ronnie Hawkins could easily fill his own book with fascinating facts and bawdry stories from a life well lived. This Arkansas-born redneck adopted Canada as his home and became one of our national musical treasures. One of his tamer tales even inspired Gordon Lightfoot to pen a song about him — "Talkin' Silver Cloud Blues," recorded by American singer-songwriter John D. Loudermilk in 1966.

The larger-than-life Hawkins loved cars and was always searching for a new ride. Cadillacs were his preferred vehicle in the late 1950s and early 1960s. But by the middle of the decade, the rock 'n' roll legend-in-the-making, who held court at Le Coq d'Or on Yonge Street in Toronto, felt it was time for an upgrade.

The story goes that Hawkins strolled into a car dealership on Bay Street sporting his trademark beard, long shaggy hair, and cowboy boots. He spotted a Rolls-Royce Silver Cloud and asked the salesman the price — after saying to the car dealer, who didn't think Hawkins could afford such a vehicle, "This RR on the front here, guess that stands for rock 'n' roll right?"

Hawkins told the salesman he wanted it and would be back. The Hawk went first to Honest Ed's for a shopping bag, and then withdrew the $18,500 needed for the Rolls and headed back to the dealership where he dumped the bag of money onto the floor. The moral of this story? Don't judge anyone by their appearance.

BRUNCH WITH JONI

In 1992, Canadian guitarist Colin Cripps was living in North Hollywood and working on the second Crash Vegas record, *Stone*. The backstory: Cripps's guitar mentor is Bill Dillon. The fellow Hamiltonian is a well-known session guy who has played with everyone from Paul Simon to Chrissie Hynde from the Pretenders. The two became good friends. In the early 1990s, when Bill split with his wife, Colin let his mentor move into the house he owned in Hamilton.

While living in L.A. that early spring in 1992, Colin called Bill frequently to check in on the house and catch up on news from home. The Crash Vegas record was two-thirds completed when Bill said he was thinking of coming out to L.A. for a visit. Over the past year, he had been

working on a record with Larry Klein, who was married to
Joni Mitchell in the early 1990s.

Bill arrived in Los Angeles and stayed in the apartment
Cripps was renting. One day, Bill called up Klein, who invited them to have brunch with him and Joni. Colin, 31
years old, was a Joni Mitchell fan, but had not yet dug deep
into her catalogue to understand what a genius she was.
He feels the encounter that followed might have been different if he went in in awe of Joni. "I was a fan, but not a
devotee," Cripps told me. "I was not awestruck by Joni then
and I think that worked in my favour. We were just a pair
of musicians hanging out. There was no fandom going on."

The foursome met in a diner in Bel Air, not far from
where Joni and Larry lived. Immediately, Cripps and Joni
connected; she asked where he was from and when he replied, "Hamilton," she shared her earliest memories of playing the Nights Two coffeehouse there back in the 1960s
and how supportive the city had been to her when she was
just starting out. Cripps recalls how she was impressed he
told her he was from Hamilton because she felt, in her experience, that people often want to be from a big city like
Toronto and won't admit the smaller town where they are
actually from.

That memorable Sunday, in that quiet diner in the foot-
hills of the Santa Monica Mountains, Joni told Colin her
life story; the guitarist recalls just how warm and open the

legendary songwriter was to him. With brunch done, Colin figured his time with Mitchell was over, but instead the couple invited him and Bill back to their house later that afternoon to hang out some more and keep the conversation going.

Thirty years on, Cripps recalls that afternoon with fondness; he only now realizes how lucky he was to have these moments with one of Canada's greatest songwriters. Mitchell had a studio set up in her Bel Air mansion. All her guitars were out in the living area, and she invited Colin to play them if he wished. In between chain-smoking American Spirit cigarettes and conversation, Joni shared a song with Cripps (including showing him the lyric sheet) that she had co-written with David Crosby called "Yvette," that would appear on the album *Turbulent Indigo* (which won a Grammy Award the following year for Best Pop Album).

"It was like being parachuted into this incredible thing that I really had no appreciation for until much later," Cripps says. "I now realize just how special this day was."

The two other details Colin shares from this April day with Joni Mitchell is that she loved Double Bubble and had a large vinyl collection. Cripps enjoyed flipping through her albums and one title especially impressed him: *Stick Around for Joy* by Icelandic alternative-rock band the Sugarcubes — the band Björk was in before going solo. "She was really hip and aware of the music of the times going on around her," Cripps says. "Joni is a significant person in my musical life and education. Later, I revisited her catalogue and discovered her genius ... I'll never forget that day."

THE ENDLESS ROACH AT THE EL MO

Toronto musician and producer Bill King shared with me this short funny story about a little-known secret stash at the El Mocambo back in the 1970s.

Long before the recent revitalization of the famous music club on Spadina Avenue in Toronto that saw merchant banker Michael Wekerle invest $30 million to reinvent the club, the El Mo was a blue-collar bar with stages on two floors. Labatt Blue and marijuana were more the flavours of the day than $12 martinis. In the downstairs dressing room, there was a wall space with a hole in the plaster where, according to King, "Everybody [all the bands in the 1970s] who played there that smoked weed or hash would stick the roach in this hole in the wall. One day, I'm there with the Jamaicans in my band and we had no weed. I said to them 'I know where there is something!' and I pried the plaster wall open and years and years of roaches came tumbling out. We rolled it up! It was no good but it was funny as hell!"

LIFE IMITATING ART ... BERGMANN

Lowest of the Low front man Ron Hawkins has been a fan of Canadian West Coast punk pioneer and rabble-rouser Art Bergmann ever since he heard the songwriter's debut solo record, *Crawl with Me,* in the late 1980s.

In 1993, Lowest of the Low (LOTL) was touring behind their successful debut record, *Shakespeare My Butt.* The four guys were crammed in a van, rolling down the Trans-Canada Highway following the white line west. Somewhere in rural Saskatchewan, Hawkins looked out the window and who did he see on the other side of the highway but his punk-rock hero. Bergmann was leaning against his guitar case, his thumb stuck out looking for a ride.

The rest of the band did not believe Hawkins, for they knew Bergmann was on the national multi-artist Big, Bad

& Groovy Tour organized by MCA Concerts. Montreal's Bootsauce was the headliner on this bill, which also featured Vancouver bands Pure and Sons of Freedom. But Bergmann, being Bergmann, had made enough enemies through the years (whether or not by his own volition or others misreading him) and the band learned after arriving at their next stop that the artist was not travelling with the rest of the touring artists. Instead, the songwriter was travelling from gig to gig by bus. When Hawkins spotted Bergmann, the musician had been kicked off a Greyhound bus for having an open bottle of wine.

Hawkins recalls how this whole strange scenario led to writing the song "Life Imitates Art" that appears on LOTL's sophomore record, *Hallucigenia*. The idea for this phrase was the anti-mimesis of Aristotle's philosophy that states it's natural for humans to make art that imitates life.

"I felt this story summed up the Canadian music industry," says Hawkins. "Here is a punk-rock genius and it was [as] if the industry was kicking him down the highway. The phrase and inspiration for the song title 'Life Imitates Art,' the gist of it came from that encounter and my observation that some of our best artists are unheralded in our time — like Van Gogh — they really only understand you after you are gone."

Hawkins references Bergmann in the song's following verse: "We all felt pretty stunned / Watching him hitch out on Highway 1 / A guitar against his elbow knowing more than they'll ever know."

Not long after this roadside incident, the band and Bergmann shared the same manager. So, when LOTL were in the studio finishing up *Hallucigenia*, Hawkins invited his songwriting hero to read the spoken word part they had planned for the song "Beer, Graffiti Walls."

A funny footnote to this story: Hawkins's song and observations on life imitating art took on even more resonance when Bergmann received the highest civilian honour — the Order of Canada — in 2020 for his "indelible contributions to the Canadian punk music scene" and his "thought-provoking discourse on social, gender and racial inequalities." Ironic, to say the least, for an anti-establishment crusader and shit disturber always trying to tear down the status quo.

86
INDEPENDENT INNOVATOR
GENTLY ROCKS TO NO. 1

Like fellow Canadian Paul Anka a decade be-
fore, Andy Kim knew he was meant to write songs. Born
Andrew Youakim, the artist was only 16 years old when he
boarded a bus on Thanksgiving weekend from his hometown of Montreal, Quebec, with just $40 in his pocket,
a cheap acoustic guitar, a couple of chords, and one original song he'd written. The destination: the famed Brill
Building — the songwriting and music-publishing hit
factory in New York City — to play this composition for
someone who might listen and offer him a songwriting contract. A bit of sweet-talking sales (and a white lie or two
from the teenager) convinced veteran songwriter Jeff Barry
to sign Kim to his Steed label and co-produce and co-write

the Canadian's first Top 20 hit, "How'd We Ever Get This Way?" which sold 800,000 copies.

The same year the famed music festival Woodstock happened in upstate New York and Kim's hometown Montreal Expos made its debut as the first team outside the United States in Major League Baseball, Kim released not just one but two huge hits: "Baby I Love You" landed in the top five, selling more than 1.5 million copies, and "Sugar, Sugar," penned for the fictional cartoon pop band the Archies to sing on the Saturday morning television show *The Archie Show*. This co-write with Barry went straight to number one (bumping off the Rolling Stones' "Honky Tonk Women") and stayed in the top spot for four weeks. It also topped the U.K. singles charts for eight weeks. The song ended 1969 as the biggest-selling record. Bob Marley even recorded a version of the song, and on February 5, 2006, "Sugar, Sugar" was inducted into the Canadian Songwriters Hall of Fame.

In the mid-'70s Kim was still writing songs, but none had the same commercial success of his earlier hits. Hoping a change of scene would help, the songwriter moved from New York to Los Angeles. The strategy worked. The very first day he landed in L.A., Kim wrote "Rock Me Gently" at 6 a.m., in only about 20 minutes. He believed in the song and knew there was something special there, but the demo he self-financed did not impress any of the record producers out West. Disenchanted with the industry, and without a record label backing him, the artist returned to Montreal where he started his own record label (Ice Records) and released the single "Rock Me Gently" independently in 1974. Kim sent the song to radio stations across the country. That's how legendary promoter and talent scout Al Cory heard the earworm on Windsor radio station CKLW The Big 8. He called Kim immediately — telling the artist he believed the song was destined to be a hit. With Cory's help, the record was distributed worldwide, and Capitol Records signed him.

"Rock Me Gently" hit the top of the charts in both Canada and the U.S., becoming the first song in history written, recorded, and released by an independent artist to achieve this feat. The song also charted in the U.K. and Ireland. "Rock Me Gently" went on to sell three million copies worldwide. When Capitol Records presented Kim with a gold record for this release, it was handed to him in the office of the record label's chairman by ex-Beatle John Lennon.

FULL MOON IN MONTREAL

In the fall of 1977, April Wine gathered at Studio Tempo in Montreal to record its seventh studio record, *First Glance*. The group, who had originally formed in Halifax in 1969, had found commercial success throughout the 1970s with such songs as "Bad Side of the Moon" and "Could Have Been a Lady." A 50-city Canadian tour the previous year had grossed over $1 million and their previous record, *The Whole World's Goin' Crazy*, reached the top spot on the domestic Billboard charts and was the first Canadian record to be shipped platinum (for sales of more than 100,000). Still, convening in La Belle Province, the band knew they could not rest on their laurels. Another hit record was needed. Terry Flood, the band's manager, negotiated a worldwide deal for the band's next record on

Capitol/EMI, which added to the pressure. *First Glance* was also the first studio record for guitarist Brian Greenway; his presence added to the heavier rock sound and direction of this recording.

April Wine lived up to the pressure and when it was released in March 1978, *First Glance* was the record that finally broke the band stateside — becoming April Wine's first gold record (sales of more than 50,000) outside Canada. The album features rockers like "Roller" (which became a Top 30 hit in the U.S. thanks to a hard-rock station in Flint, Michigan, that put it into heavy rotation) and "Rock N' Roll Is a Vicious Game." Here's a funny story shared by band founder Myles Goodwyn about the recording of the radio-friendly piano ballad "Comin' Right Down on Top of Me."

> We were recording the song live at Tempo Studios in Montreal. The song is a slow, bluesy number. Our drummer Jerry Mercer was in the sound booth and I was in the studio recording the track on the piano. I was nearly done playing the song when I looked over to the control room to let them know I was coming to the end of the song. Instead of our engineer or Jerry, what did I see reflecting back at me from the glassed-in mixing booth

but four derrières! I could not believe it. There was a line of four guys with their pants down mooning me! I was not expecting this at all and for a short second it frazzled me as I paused and hit an unplanned chord. Then, I smiled and started the final verse again to finish the song properly. If you listen to the recording of this song today, you can hear that hesitation and my impromptu tag line at the end of the song. As I stood up from the piano, and the engineer pressed stop in the control room, all I could hear was explosive laughter and applause.

Who were these bare-assed men behind these full moons in Montreal? Scottish rockers Nazareth, good friends of April Wine, who were in town recording as well. Years later, Goodwyn got revenge on these merry pranksters when April Wine was on tour with Nazareth. "They had a version of 'Cocaine' that they played and during that song I had rigged it up so that flour reigned down over the front of the stage to make it look like it was snowing cocaine. Then, at the appropriate moment, I strolled across the stage wearing nothing but a towel and reading a newspaper."

CAN I GET A HALLELUJAH?

Did you know that before Leonard Cohen rose to fame as a songwriter with such Canadian classics and oft-covered tunes as "Suzanne," "Sisters of Mercy," and "Hallelujah," he was a poet and published author — having penned four volumes of poetry and a pair of novels, *The Favourite Game* and *Beautiful Losers*? For those that do not know Cohen's deep catalogue as one of our country's revered songwriters, even they most likely recognize "Hallelujah" due to it showing up in many TV shows and movies. The song has also become an anthem at weddings, church services, and state funerals for its waltz-like rhythms and a melody that is at once both sombre and joyful. It's hard to believe this song was not even a single when it appeared as the opening song on Side B of the artist's *Various Positions* album. Cohen's version of "Hallelujah" only charted on Billboard's Hot 100 in the month following the artist's death in 2016, when it reached the top five in digital sales.

Here is the long and winding journey of how this song, which was inducted into the Canadian Songwriters Hall of Fame in 2006, went from a forgotten track to a ubiquitous song that rejuvenated Cohen's career.

The final recorded version of "Hallelujah" put to tape in 1984 had only four verses, but Cohen wrote as many as 80 verses — filling notebooks with rewrites — until he was satisfied with it. Despite its name, "Hallelujah" is not an ode to any religious deity, but rather a declaration by Cohen of his faith in life and love. The song tries to navigate the worlds between desire and spiritualism, hinting at humans' dark side. Like many of Cohen's works, it's filled with obscurity. Scholars and critics alike have debated about its meaning for decades and one can find new interpretations on each subsequent listen.

When it was finally finished and recorded, Cohen's producer John Lissauer, thinking they had a single, took it to Columbia president Walter Yetnikoff, who was not sold. He famously asked Cohen and Lissauer: "What is this? This isn't pop music. We're not releasing it. This is a disaster." The song was buried, and few heard this deep cut from *Various Positions*.

Flash ahead four years. Bob Dylan got the song and loved it and started to include it in his sets. Then in 1991, John Cale covered "Hallelujah" with a wistful piano version on the Cohen tribute record *I'm Your Fan*. Suddenly, the song was getting traction — seven years after its release. Finally, in 1994, came Jeff Buckley's otherworldly version on his debut, *Grace*, which added an additional verse. As the 2000s dawned, the song kept getting synched in movies and TV shows. First, and what made it become a huge hit, was that it showed up in the DreamWorks blockbuster *Shrek*. Later in the 2000s, the song ended up on one hit TV drama after another, including *Scrubs*, *The West Wing*, *The O.C.*, *House*, *Without a Trace*, and *ER*. *Maclean's* magazine once said "Hallelujah" is "the closest thing pop music has to a sacred text." In 2022, there was even a documentary made — not on Cohen — but specifically on the song's road from obscurity to über-famous (*Hallelujah: Leonard Cohen, a Journey, a Song*).

Cohen was amused that other artists found more success covering "Hallelujah" than the poet and songwriter himself did from his original version. In 2004, *Rolling Stone* stated it was one of the greatest songs ever recorded; in 2013, the U.S. Library of Congress added Buckley's version to the National Recording Registry. By 2010, the song that Columbia had rejected back in 1984 was so ubiquitous that Cohen even got tired of it, saying in an interview that "it's a good song ... but I think people oughta stop singing it for a while."

A HANDSOME AND "HAPPY ACCIDENT"

During the mid-1980s, Toronto's Queen Street West was a hangout for musicians, art students, and bohemians. There was a real DIY ethos in this arts scene that spawned many acts like Parachute Club, Mary Margaret O'Hara, and the Cowboy Junkies. The clubs in this block included the legendary Horseshoe Tavern, the BamBoo, the Rivoli, and the Cameron House. If there was a king of this Queen Street West scene it was Handsome Ned.

Born Robin Masyk, Handsome Ned was a cowpunk pioneer who held court at the Cameron, doing a matinee every Saturday for five years. On June 27, 1985, Blue Rodeo played a showcase gig at the Horseshoe Tavern with Handsome Ned opening. Doug McClement set up his 24-track recording truck to capture the Blue Rodeo show with Terry Brown at the helm to produce the live recording. The idea was that this live tape would help seal the deal and land the country-rockers a record deal with Warner Brothers. The crew also decided to record the opening act. Unfortunately, Ned refused to pay the recording costs for his portion of the two-inch tapes, so former Horseshoe owner X-Ray MacRae kept the tapes and stored them at his farmhouse in Napanee, Ontario.

A decade after Handsome Ned's unfortunate death from a suspected drug overdose on January 10, 1987, Ned's brother Jim Masyk and MacRae met by chance at an ATM in Toronto. MacRae donated the tapes to the Masyk family, who had McClement bake them and clean them up. The result: A six-song EP released by Cameron House Records in 2016 called *The Handsome Neds: Live at the Horseshoe*, which provided a glimpse into Handsome Ned's rockabilly genius for a whole new generation to enjoy.

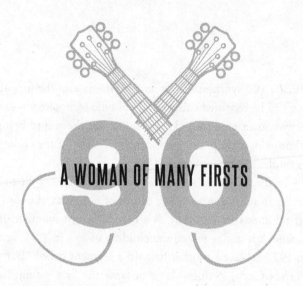

A WOMAN OF MANY FIRSTS

Canadian Cree artist Buffy Sainte-Marie is known for penning such classics as "Universal Soldier," "Until It's Time for You to Go," and "Up Where We Belong." The artist and activist is a trailblazer both in the way she recorded music and in her actions. Though she started out as a folk singer, playing coffee houses and clubs in New York's Greenwich Village, Sainte-Marie was not one to stay put in any genre for long and was always looking for ways to take her music and art in new directions, whether it was through the instrumentation she incorporated or new technology with which she experimented in the studio.

In 1969, Sainte-Marie, 28, released her sixth record, *Illuminations*. What made this album significant is that it was the first record to feature vocals processed through a

Buchla 100 synthesizer. *Illuminations* was also the first album to be recorded using quadraphonic technology — an early cousin of surround sound. Despite the record being a commercial flop, it is now considered one of the earliest examples of electronic music.

In the 1970s, Sainte-Marie also turned for a while to a career in television; over the course of five years, the songwriter appeared regularly as a recurring cast member on *Sesame Street*. She joined the children's show in 1975, and in 1977 achieved another first. In a segment called "Buffy Nurses Cody," Sainte-Marie became the first woman in history to breastfeed on national television when she breastfed her son Dakota "Cody" Starblanket Wolfchild while talking to Big Bird about how natural and normal this practice is for many mothers.

As if that is not enough firsts for this amazing artist, in 1982, Sainte-Marie became the first Indigenous person to win an Oscar when her song "Up Where We Belong," co-written for the film *An Officer and a Gentleman*, won an Academy Award for Best Original Song. Finally, in 1992, Sainte-Marie made her first album in 16 years, *Coincidence and Likely Stories*. And you guessed it — the album signified another first for the artist — the first album made over the internet. She signed with English label Ensign but did not wish to travel to London to record with producer Chris Burkett. Instead, though the internet was still in its infancy, the pair came up with a plan to share MIDI files with each other and build them byte by byte despite being oceans apart.

TRIUMPH'S TEXAS TRIUMPH

The year: 1977. Canadian rock trio Triumph (Rik Emmett, Mike Levine, and Gil Moore) had released their major-label self-titled debut the year before and it went gold in Canada — selling more than 50,000 copies. At that time radio stations played a pivotal role in a band's success and DJs held a lot of power and influence to expand a band's reach. Triumph did not have a U.S. record deal, so all of their records stateside were imported from Canada. Thanks to one DJ in San Antonio, Texas, Triumph found success in the Lone Star State. KISS-FM in the Alamo City started to spin the band's sophomore release, *Rock & Roll Machine*, which contained a cover version of Joe Walsh's "Rocky Mountain Way." Listeners loved the Canadian rockers. Suddenly, radio stations in other major Texas markets like Houston also began playing them.

The band was still mainly playing bars and clubs in Canada at this time. Then, due to Sammy Hagar pulling out of a multi-band gig in San Antonio at the 5,000-seat Municipal Auditorium, a promoter extended an invitation to Triumph to play after seeing the band's local popularity. The challenge was getting the band's pyrotechnic light show equipment and visas in order in time to play the gig. But the band figured it out and on February 18, 1977, the Canadian power trio made their U.S. debut, headlining the triple bill to a sold-out crowd of 5,500 in downtown San Antonio. They were a huge hit.

Texans' love affair with Triumph never waned. In 1983, the City of San Antonio presented the band with the Emissary of the Muses Award outside the Alamo. The award was basically like giving the Canadians the key to the city. In an interview in 2022 with the *San Antonio Current* reflecting on what the city meant to Triumph, Mike Levine said that it was "our second home."

92

YOUTUBE LAUNCHES THE STRATFORD KID

In 2007, a boy from Stratford, Ontario, just shy of becoming a teenager, created a YouTube channel with the help of his mom. The reason: so his extended family could see his performances. Who's the kid? Just some guy you might have heard of named Justin Bieber.

The channel was named Kidrauhl and the initial videos were of Bieber singing in a talent show. Bieber was not looking for fame. YouTube was in its infancy and Bieber became infatuated with the new online platform. The teenager started posting more and more content. The earliest Kidrauhl videos were of Bieber with his guitar performing covers of songs by the likes of Lil' Bow Wow, Sarah McLachlan, and Alicia Keys in his bedroom. Suddenly the views to his channel exploded. Comments were posted from strangers requesting more videos and songs. Somehow, this Stratford kid became the number one most subscribed YouTube channel in Canada and 20th in the world. The media started calling. First, the Biebers received an email from tabloid TV talk show host Maury Povich wanting him to do a song as part of a competition on his show. Justin's mom vetoed this request. The calls did not stop. Next were managers and music industry people offering him deals. One of these was record executive and talent manager Scooter Braun, who discovered a video of Bieber busking outside the Stratford Festival by accident while searching for another singer. Braun was sold and tracked Bieber down. He eventually convinced Bieber's mom to allow the teenager to meet him in Atlanta, Georgia, to record some demos. Both Justin Timberlake and Usher were also interested in signing the teenage star-in-the-making. Bieber hired Braun as his manager and the 14-year-old inked a record deal with Island/Def Jam in 2008. The following year the teen idol released his debut EP, *My World*. How he found his original success never stopped giving back. In 2019, Bieber became the first artist to surpass 45 million YouTube subscribers.

TRAIL-BLAZING TRANSGENDER SOUL SINGER

Imagine you were born Black and transgender in Nashville, Tennessee, in 1940 — a time when the southern United States was still segregated and teeming with racism. This was the beginning for R&B artist Jackie Shane.

Never afraid to show her true identity, Shane wore makeup and jewellery to school in her formative years and was a natural performer. Still, the American South of her youth was not the safest place for a transgender Black person. Shane moved to Canada, which became her adopted home for decades.

The pioneering transgender R&B artist settled in Montreal, where she connected with trumpet player and bandleader Frank Motley. The pair formed the R&B group Motley Crew. In 1959, Shane relocated the band to Toronto.

Throughout the early to mid-1960s, she played regularly on the bustling Yonge Street club circuit — performing to sold-out crowds at places like the Saphire Tavern and helping to create what later came to be known as the Toronto Sound.

Shane never recorded a studio album as she distrusted music labels but had a hit with a cover of William Bell's "Any Other Way," which reached No. 2 on the CHUM singles chart in 1963. Funk innovator and Rock and Roll Hall of Fame member George Clinton even tried to convince her to join his band Parliament-Funkadelic, and Motown and Atlantic Records both tried to sign Shane. Instead, she retired from music in 1971 and returned to the United States, first to Los Angeles to care for her ailing mother and then back to Nashville.

In recent years, Shane's legacy and importance as a trailblazer in queer visibility and the Toronto sound of the 1960s has received renewed interest. A life-size mural of the singer was painted on Yonge Street in 2016, and before she passed away in 2019, a project featuring some of her old recordings received a Grammy nomination for best historical album. A *Heritage Minute* was created about Shane's life in 2023.

BETTING THE HOUSE ON THE GUESS WHO

Before recording some of the biggest rock 'n' roll songs of the 1970s, Jack Richardson was an account executive with advertising agency McCann-Erickson in the mid-1960s. The Coca-Cola Company was one of his main clients, and he created many successful campaigns for the soft-drink maker with Canadian artists like David Clayton-Thomas, Bobby Curtola, and the Guess Who.

From the moment he heard the Guess Who, Richardson saw the huge potential of the band from Winnipeg. He acquired the band's contract from Quality Records for $1,000 and signed them to his newly created company (Nimbus 9 Productions), which he founded in 1968 with three partners. Richardson believed in the rockers so much that he took out a second mortgage on his house to finance the recording of the band's fourth studio record, *Wheatfield Soul.*

Talk about taking a gamble: Richardson was in his early forties and had five kids. But the risk paid off. Released in 1969, the piano rock ballad "These Eyes" — the first single from *Wheatfield Soul* — went to No. 7 in Canada on the RPM Charts and No. 1 on the CHUM radio charts and helped land the band a U.S. deal with RCA Records. It was the first single by the Guess Who to achieve gold status for sales of more than one million copies. The gold record was presented to the band on the popular show *American Bandstand.* The song was also a Top 10 hit south of the border and was inducted in 2005 into the Canadian Songwriters Hall of Fame.

Richardson went on to produce the band's U.S. and Canadian number one single "American Woman" in 1970, which made the Guess Who the bestselling rock group in the world that year. Today, the Juno Award for Producer of the Year is named after Richardson.

BEWARE THE HUMAN SERVIETTE

Sporting his signature Scottish Tam, tartan pants, and goofy glasses, Nardwuar is one of the music industry's most feared — and now most famous — interviewers due to his extensive research and unmatched curiosity about his subjects.

Born John Ruskin, "Nardwuar" learned his adept reporting skills and his love of storytelling by observing his mom, Olga, who hosted a Vancouver show called *Our Pioneers and Neighbours* in the 1970s and early 1980s. Ruskin's first interview was during high school when he booked bands as a member of the student council. The inaugural interviewees were Art Bergmann and Tom Upex of Vancouver punk band Poisoned, who sat down with the teenager after playing a school dance.

In 1986, while studying history as an undergrad at the University of British Columbia, Ruskin changed his on-air name to Nardwuar, the Human Serviette, when he started volunteering with the campus FM radio station CiTR. Where did the name come from? *Nardwuar Presents* was put on posters for punk rock shows he and a group of friends promoted during his high-school days in West Vancouver. The made-up word was an inside joke the buddies came up with to refer to old people. The Human Serviette phrase, according to Ruskin, is just another dumb name he created: "Human" coming from the Cramps' song "Human Fly" and "Serviette" to distinguish himself as Canadian since in the U.S. they do not use this French word, but rather "napkins." Initially, CiTR only gave Nardwuar one minute of airtime. But he was persistent and eventually landed his own show, which is now one of the longest running on Canadian campus radio — having been on air every Friday afternoon since 1987.

Early in his broadcast career, Nardwuar established his reputation as someone celebrities feared getting grilled by since he asked tough questions. His first question is always "Who are you?" He also got to be known as a "guerrilla journalist" for his habit of sneaking into press conferences and confronting political leaders and non-music celebrities with confusing questions. Not surprising, over the decades, Nardwuar's eccentric interviewing style has not gone over well with everyone. One famous example is Canadian Sebastian Bach (Skid Row's lead singer), who stole Nardwuar's favourite toque and smashed the interview tape after being angered by the journalist's questions.

In a 2008 MuchMusic interview, record producer and American songwriter Pharrell Williams complimented Nardwuar on how thorough his homework was, calling it "second to none." The journalist closes all his interviews with this pair of phrases: "Keep on rockin' in the free world" and "Doot doola doot doot doo" and then puts the mic in the face of his subject and gets them to retort: "Doot doo." This sound was what he heard the organist play at Vancouver Canuck hockey games during his formative years. For more than three and a half decades, Nardwuar has had questions (both insightful and bizarre) for everyone from Alice Cooper and Lizzo to Snoop Dogg.

On September 29, 2019, Vancouver's mayor declared it Nardwuar Day when the hometown broadcast legend was inducted into the B.C. Entertainment Hall of Fame.

DUTCH LOVE

96

From Holland to Toronto with plenty of stops in between, for 50 years songwriter-producer Vince DeGiorgio has followed the song. The road began in clubs when DeGiorgio was an underage DJ making $40 an hour to support his record-buying habit. He penned his first lyrics as a teen and later took a turn as an A&R representative for RCA — signing NSYNC to their first major-label deal for North America and introducing Justin Timberlake to the world. DeGiorgio's journey is as diverse as the artists with whom he's co-written songs. He has had chart-topping hits in six different countries, his works have been recorded in 11 different languages, and his songs have sold 30 million records.

According to DeGiorgio, the "weirdest thing" in his career started back in 1983, when his first co-collaboration song, "My Forbidden Lover," hit the number two spot on the dance charts in the Netherlands. More than twenty years later, the songwriter was out of his publishing deal with BMG when an intern introduced him to David Schreurs — another songwriter in Amsterdam. The connection was immediate. For the next 18 months the pair co-wrote a ton of songs together. Then, one night in 2006, they settled in to write at 2 a.m. and magic happened. Schreurs shared an idea and DeGiorgio responded with a riff that he says was as if he was "writing for Billie Holiday." The resulting song, "Back It Up," arrived in 90 minutes. The pair decided to make a demo and get someone to sing it. When the original singer didn't show up, a then relatively unknown Dutch singer, Caro Emerald, took her place ... and nailed it. The pair knew they had a smash in the making and released the single independently. The song exploded in the Netherlands. Schreurs convinced DeGiorgio that they needed to make an album with this Dutch singer. The songs flowed and the result, *Deleted Scenes from the Cutting Room Floor*, was released January 29, 2010, in the Netherlands. The pair penned the second single, "A Night Like This," in 25 minutes. The lyrics were inspired by the 1967 James Bond flick *Casino Royale*. It was one of the last songs to make the record, but this was the big hit. The song went on to sell more than two million copies and based on it, Emerald sold out Royal Albert Hall not just once, but twice.

Incredibly, 22 years after landing his first hit in the Netherlands, DeGiorgio had another one. "A Night Like This" reached the top spot on the Dutch Top 100 singles charts and No. 2 on the Dutch Top 40 and was the 2010 Song of the Year in the Netherlands. It also hit the number one position in Poland, Austria, and Romania. The record was never released in North America, but it changed DeGiorgio's life. The song was used in the sixth episode of season three of *Pretty Little Liars* and has also been used in advertising campaigns for Martini, Wrigley, and Nestlé.

CANADA'S FIRST COUNTRY MUSIC STAR

In 1994, two years before he passed away at age 91, Wilf Carter, known as the "father of Canadian country and western music," gathered the members of his band who were still alive and toured the prairies in his old silver Cadillac convertible — a tour that became known as The Last Roundup.

Nicknamed and known initially in the United States as Montana Slim — a name a secretary came up with while typing the lyrics to one of his earliest songs to differentiate him from the Carter Family — Wilf Carter was born one of nine children in Port Hilford, Nova Scotia, in 1904. At 15 years old he left home and took on odd jobs, including working as a lumberjack. A few years later, the young man boarded a train for Alberta, heading west for work.

There, Carter first found fame in Banff playing guitar and yodelling for tourists and became known as "the Yodelling Cowboy." He picked up a variety of jobs — from a cowboy horse wrangler to singing on trail rides for well-to-dos through the Rocky Mountains.

Carter approached local Calgary station CFCN and asked for a gig. It took a couple of tries, and in 1930 he performed his first broadcast. Word spread of his talent, and he eventually found a national audience with his unique high and lonesome voice. This led to recording his first demos at RCA Studios in Montreal, one of the earliest recording studios in North America. The pair of originals he recorded were "My Swiss Moonlight Lullaby" and "The Capture of Albert Johnson," the latter based on the real-life hunt for the Mad Trapper of the northwest. RCA Victor released these singles in 1934 and they became the first hit record ever by a Canadian country performer. For a while, Carter settled in Calgary and was a trailblazer in building up the country music industry in Alberta's largest city. In 1985, the founding father of country music was inducted into the Canadian Music Hall of Fame.

98 THE BIRTH OF MARIPOSA

One night in 1961, Ruth Jones of Orillia heard a talk about tourism and small towns and was struck with a desire to create an event that would bring tourism dollars to her Ontario town. Ruth and her husband, Casey, loved music and often headed south on the weekends to Toronto to attend the coffee houses and folk clubs there. With just a small grant of $250 from the Orillia town council and relying on her savings (and a mortgage on the family home) for the rest of the investment, Jones and local alderman and broadcaster Pete McGarvey created the Mariposa Folk Festival — after getting advice from the organizers of the Newport Folk Festival, which, at the time, was the only other major folk festival in North America. The Mariposa Folk Festival was named after the fictional town modelled on Orillia from Stephen Leacock's famous satirical novel *Sunshine Sketches of a Little Town*. The first logo and posters were designed by Ian Tyson, who went on to become one of the country's most famed folk singer-songwriters.

On August 18, 1961, more than 5,000 folk lovers arrived in Orillia for the inaugural Mariposa Folk Festival, which included folk groups the Travellers and Ian & Sylvia. Gordon Lightfoot, an Orillia native, who was performing at the time as a duo with Terry Whelan, was not invited to the inaugural festival as organizers considered them "too commercial." But the second year of the festival Lightfoot and Whelan were booked and were a hit. By its third year, Mariposa had grown by word of mouth, and the town of 15,000 saw an estimated 20,000 to 30,000 descend upon it. As a result, the town council banned the festival from taking place within the city limits the following year.

Today, the Mariposa Folk Festival is still going strong. In 2022, it celebrated its 60th anniversary (following two years of cancellations due to the Covid-19 pandemic) with a stacked lineup that featured Blue Rodeo, Mavis Staples, Blackie and the Rodeo Kings, and Lennon Stella. A highlight was on the Sunday afternoon when Lightfoot was inducted into the Mariposa Hall of Fame.

ALL ABOARD THE YOUNG TRAIN

This whole book could be written with fascinating facts about Canada's musical chameleon Neil Young. One fact you might not know is that the Rock and Roll Hall of Fame musician is a model train enthusiast and has had an obsession with collecting model trains since he was a kid.

Young's hobby of collecting high-end Lionel trains started back in the 1970s when he bought his first Lionel passenger train at a shop on Sunset Boulevard. In a 2012 interview with David Letterman, Young discussed how his interest in model trains first began: "It's just relaxing. I was shopping once, Christmas shopping, back in 1977 or '78, maybe '76 … I was shopping for presents, and I found this huge Lionel thing, and it was like many thousands of dollars. I thought, my goodness, this is very expensive. Being a rich hippie, I bought it immediately."

His first collection and train track layout was on the dining-room table at home in Los Angeles, which he set up as a way of connecting with his son Zeke, who has cerebral palsy. Young's second son Ben, a quadriplegic, also enjoyed spending time with his dad and the trains.

Later, as his train obsession grew, Young created what he called the "train barn" on his northern California ranch. This was no ordinary model railroad. The 2,800-square-foot barn featured 750-feet of track and included tunnels and buildings for his vast collection of vintage Lionel trains — pre-war and postwar locomotives, along with freight and passenger cars — to explore. Surrounding the tracks was a natural landscape of Mother Nature's bounty that included ferns, boulders, trees, billboards, and even a pond with real goldfish. At one time, Young even had his engineers rig the phones in the barn so a train whistle announced his incoming calls. The train barn was a place for the musician to escape from the world of music that consumed so much of his life. It's apparent that he bought into the Lionel Trains tag line from a 1934 ad that told consumers: "Lionel makes a boy feel like a man and a man feel like a boy."

In 1992, further inspired by his sons and wanting to give them a gift that would help them and others enjoy his hobby of model trains, the artist launched Liontech with former Lionel Trains Inc. owner Richard Kughn. The research and development company created and built the TrainMaster Command Control (TMCC) system for O scale three-rail model and toy trains. The invention allowed operators to control their trains by remote control and gave the toy trains realistic digitized sounds; the TMCC also introduced new features like whistle, bell, chugging, diesel roar, electro-couplers, and the ability to turn RailSounds on or off. Young's collection of Lionel model trains was so impressive that in 2017 he auctioned more than 230 pieces from his personal collection of Lionel Trains for $300,000.

HAIRDRESSERS AND BIG HAIR BANDS

Formed in Toronto in 1979, Platinum Blonde began as a tribute act to the Police, playing bars around their hometown. The glam punk and big hair new wave band later found commercial success with their catchy originals in the MuchMusic era of the 1980s. In 1983, after the release of their debut, *Standing in the Dark*, videos for songs like "Doesn't Really Matter" and "Standing in the Dark" made these bleach-blond rockers household names. Both songs were nominated in the new Juno category in 1984 for Video of the Year. Two of the members of the multi-platinum selling Platinum Blonde cut hair to earn a living before becoming professional musicians. Kenny MacLean, bassist and keyboardist in the band, was a former hairdresser and even had a band called the Hairdressers

before joining Platinum Blonde. Lead singer Mark Holmes
also spent time working in a salon. The band's name came
from the fact that all the members had platinum blond hair
that — you guessed it — Holmes gave them.

FROM DANCING QUEEN TO BILLBOARD CHARTER

Before she became an internet sensation, a pop idol, and a Juno Award nominee for Breakthrough Artist of the Year, Tate McRae had her 15 minutes of fame for her dance moves rather than her singing chops. Long before she started to sing, McRae's passion was dance. She was six years old when she started attending the Alberta Ballet and trained 11 hours a day. Dedicated? Definitely.

At 11 years old, McRae was awarded a two-week scholarship at the Berlin State Ballet after winning the silver medal at the 2015 Youth America Grand Prix — the world's largest student ballet competition. In 2016, the Calgary-born McRae was a backup dancer for Justin Bieber's *Purpose* World Tour. That same year she made an appearance on

The Ellen DeGeneres Show as a member of DancerPalooza. The pièce de résistance came during the 13th season of the American reality TV show *So You Think You Can Dance* when the 13-year-old finished in third place. During her audition for the show, after performing a backwards walkover, judge Paula Abdul called her "a gift from god."

The connection to Bieber is apropos. McRae used the same formula the Stratford kid had used to launch his career. Despite still feeling uncertain about her career path and whether dance was the way to go, McRae felt a pull from another passion she had kept hidden — at least from the public — singing. After appearing on *So You Think You Can Dance*, McRae set up a YouTube channel called Create with Tate. The original idea: it was a place to share her dance choreography. About a month into filming, she lost footage for her weekly post, so McRae decided to upload an original song she'd written instead. She once told an interviewer that she had no idea where this song came from and called it "an accident." The piano ballad "One Day," went on to be viewed more than 39 million times.

This happy accident eventually led to not just one, but 11 record labels vying to sign the Canadian. She ended up signing with RCA. Oh, and her first official single after signing a deal was a song written by Billie Eilish and her brother Finneas, "Tear Myself Apart." What broke McRae — and took her career to another level — was one of her originals,

"You Broke Me First." The pop song, released April 17, 2020, exploded on TikTok; it was seen in over a million videos. It ended up being the second most streamed song by a female artist in 2020 and has been streamed on Spotify more than one billion times. The song hit the eighth spot on the Canadian Hot 100 and cracked the Top 10 in 10 other countries. In 2021, she was the youngest musician featured in *Forbes*'s 30 Under 30 list. These days McRae is dancing her way to the bank and into the hearts and minds of music lovers worldwide; she's a true triple threat.

ACKNOWLEDGEMENTS

My vocation as a music journalist began at Western University in the early 1990s when I contributed to the *Gazette* (the daily student newspaper). I never imagined that some of the artists I interviewed as a nervous college reporter and entertainment editor back then would become friends 30 years later. Or, that I would publish a pair of books on two of Canada's most revered concert venues. I am grateful to my publisher and to my family — especially my wife, Patricia — for allowing me to achieve these dreams. About six months after my *Massey Hall* book was published, I was brainstorming about my next book when Kathryn Lane, Dundurn's associate publisher, pitched me this idea. In 2019, Dundurn published *101 Fascinating Hockey Facts*, authored by Brian McFarlane, and were considering developing a series of these titles. It did not take long for me to agree. My son said I was selling out and my wife told people that this was my "bathroom book." Jokes aside, I'm humbled and honoured that once again Dundurn believed in my abilities and trusted me to take on this project. Thanks to Kwame, Kathryn, Chris, Elena, Alyssa, Karen (love the cover!) and the small but mighty Dundurn team — past and present. Special thanks to editor Carrie Gleason for tightening my prose, narrowing the focus, coming up with catchy titles, and finding the fascinating fact within a story when it was not evident.

Finally, thanks to the artists and music industry colleagues who took time to share their fascinating stories. A special thank you to the following for granting me free permission to reprint selected lyrics to one of their songs: Geoffrey Kelly, Ron Hawkins, Lorraine Segato, Ivan Doroschuk, and Corin Raymond.

ABOUT THE AUTHOR

Photos by Holly

Ever since David McPherson attended his first rock concert, the Who in 1989, and bought his first LP, *Freeze Frame* by the J. Geils Band, music has been the elixir of his life. David shared this passion in his two previous bestselling books: *The Legendary Horseshoe Tavern* and *Massey Hall*. A current contributor to *Words & Music*, *Amplify*, and Grammy.com, David's byline has also appeared in the *Toronto Star*, the *Globe and Mail*, *Paste*, *American Songwriter*, *No Depression*, and *Canadian Musician*. As a freelance writer and corporate communicator, David helps his clients get the words right. He lives in Waterloo, Ontario.